THE ZULU WAR JOURNAL

BY
COLONEL
HENRY HARFORD, C.B.

Pen & Sword
MILITARY

This edition published in 2014 by

Pen & Sword Military
An imprint of
Pen & Sword Books Ltd
47 Church Street
Barnsley
South Yorkshire
S70 2AS

Copyright © Coda Books Ltd.
Published under licence by Pen & Sword Books Ltd.

ISBN: 9781783462513

A CIP catalogue record for this book is available from the British Library

All rights reserved. No part of this book may be reproduced or transmitted in any form or by any means, electronic or mechanical including photocopying, recording or by any information storage and retrieval system, without permission from the Publisher in writing.

Printed and bound in England
By CPI Group (UK) Ltd, Croydon, CR0 4YY

Pen & Sword Books Ltd incorporates the imprints of Pen & Sword Aviation, Pen & Sword Family History, Pen & Sword Maritime, Pen & Sword Military, Pen & Sword Discovery, Pen & Sword Politics, Pen & Sword Atlas, Pen & Sword Archaeology, Wharncliffe Local History, Wharncliffe True Crime, Wharncliffe Transport, Pen & Sword Select, Pen & Sword Military Classics, Leo Cooper, The Praetorian Press, Claymore Press, Remember When, Seaforth Publishing and Frontline Publishing

For a complete list of Pen & Sword titles please contact
PEN & SWORD BOOKS LIMITED
47 Church Street, Barnsley, South Yorkshire, S70 2AS, England
E-mail: enquiries@pen-and-sword.co.uk
Website: www.pen-and-sword.co.uk

CONTENTS

INTRODUCTION 4
by Bob Carruthers

CHAPTER 1
PREPARATIONS FOR WAR 15

CHAPTER 2
ISANDHLWANA 31

CHAPTER 3
RORKE'S DRIFT 54

CHAPTER 4
RECOVERY OF THE QUEEN'S COLOUR 71

CHAPTER 5
RETURN TO THE 99TH REGIMENT 86

CHAPTER 6
THE CAPTURE OF CETEWAYO 100

INTRODUCTION

THE ANGLO-ZULU WAR was fought in 1879 between the British Empire and the Zulu Kingdom. Following a campaign by which Lord Carnarvon had successfully brought about federation in Canada, it was thought that similar policy embracing a combined military and political campaign might succeed with the African kingdoms, tribal areas and Boer republics in South Africa. Accordingly in 1874, Sir Henry Bartle Frere was sent to South Africa as High Commissioner for the British Empire to bring those plans to fruition. Among the obstacles in his path however were the presence of the independent states of the South African Republic and the Kingdom of Zululand with its fearsome army of 35,000 warriors.

Bartle Frere, acting on his own initiative and without the approval of the British government sought to bring about a war with the Zulu. Without informing London he presented an ultimatum on 11th December 1878, to the Zulu king Cetshwayo. Bartle Frere was well aware that the Zulu king could not possibly comply with the ultimatum which was obviously designed to precipitate war. Predictably Cetshwayo did not comply and Bartle Frere proactively desptached Lord Chelmsford to invade Zululand.

The war is notable for several particularly bloody battles, including a startling and unexpected opening victory by the Zulu at Isandhlwana which was the largest British military defeat of the Victorian era. Inevitably however he war soon swung in favour of the British and eventually resulted in a British victory which marked the end of the Zulu nation's independence.

For an event which took place in an age of almost universal literacy good primary source accounts of the Zulu War of 1879 are surprisingly rare. One excellent primary source is the one you now hold in your hands. This is the journal of Colonel Henry Charles Harford C.B. who saw action as a young man in the Zulu War of 1879. He served a Staff Officer to Commandant Lonsdale of the 3rd Regiment, Natal Native Contingent (N.N.C.). Harford kept a journal throughout the war in which he recorded his experiences and original observations. Today this manuscript represents a rare and valuable contribution to the historiography of the campaign.

It is interesting to note that in 1878 at the time when the road to war was developing Harford actually held a British Army commission with the rank of Lieutenant in the 99th regiment, but, having spent his youth in Natal, he possessed a thorough knowledge of the country and the Zulu language. In consequence as the war clouds continued to gather he resigned from the 99th Regiment and was appointed to the N.N.C. and given the honorary rank of Captain, a role in which he made himself very useful to the Contingent as the events of the war unfolded.

This interesting record of the campaign from unusual angle allows modern audiences a rare insight into the campaign from a rare and often overlooked perspective. The N.N.C. played an important role in the events of the war and in his journal Harford provides a vivid and compelling eye witness account of some of the most famous incidents of the war.

The pretext for the war had its origins in border disputes between the Zulu leader, Cetshwayo, and the Boers in the Transvaal region. Following a commission enquiry on the border dispute which reported in favour of the Zulu nation in July 1878, Sir Henry Bartle Frere, acting on his own, added an ultimatum to the commission meeting, much to the surprise of the Zulu representatives who then relayed it to Cetshwayo. The most far reaching and patently unpalatable British demand was that the Zulu army be disbanded and the men allowed to go home. Bartle Frere was bent upon breaking the Zulu king's power and this was further evidenced by the demand that the Zulu military system should be discontinued and other military regulations adopted, to be decided upon after consultation with the Great Council and British Representatives and that every man should be free to marry. Other unacceptable demands included the perfunctory demand that all missionaries and their converts, who until 1877 had lived in Zululand, should be allowed to return and reoccupy their stations and these missionaries should be allowed to teach and any Zulu, who henceforth were to be free to listen to their teaching. A British Agent was also to be allowed to reside in Zululand, in order to see that the provisions were carried out. Cetshwayo had not responded by the end of the year 1878, so an extension was granted by Bartle Frere until 11th January 1879. Cetshwayo returned no answer to the preposterous demands of Bartle Frere by the 11th January 1879, and accordingly, without the authorisation of the British Government, a British force under Lieutenant General Frederick Augustus Thesiger, 2nd Baron Chelmsford invaded Zululand.

Lord Chelmsford, as the Commander-in-Chief of British forces during the war, was concerned that the Zulus would avoid battle and he initially planned an elaborate five-pronged invasion of Zululand composed of over 15,000 troops in five columns and designed to encircle the Zulu army and force it to fight. In the event, Chelmsford settled on three invading columns. With the days to the final deadline counting down he moved with his troops from Pietermaritzburg to a forward camp at Helpmekar. On 9th January 1879 the British moved to Rorke's Drift, and early on 11th January commenced crossing the Buffalo River into Zululand. Three columns were to invade Zululand, from the Lower Tugela, Rorke's Drift, and Utrecht respectively, their objective being to converge upon Ulundi, the royal capital.

While Cetshwayo's army numbered perhaps 35,000 men, it was essentially an untrained militia force which could be called out in time of national danger. It had a very limited logistical capacity and could only stay in the field a few weeks before the troops would be obliged to return to their civilian duties. Zulu warriors were armed primarily with Assegai thrusting spears, known in Zulu as *iklwa*, clubs, some throwing spears and shields made of cowhide. These weapons were clearly no match for a modern army equipped with the rapid firing Martini-Henry Mark 2, a breech-loading single-shot lever-actuated rifle.

The initial entry of all three columns was unopposed. On 22 January the centre column, which had advanced from Rorke's Drift, was encamped near Isandhlwana; on the morning of that day Lord Chelmsford split his forces and moved out to support a reconnoitring party, leaving the camp in charge of Colonel Pulleine. The British were outmanoeuvred by the main Zulu army nearly 20,000 strong led by Ntshingwayo kaMahole Khoza. Chelmsford was lured eastward with much of his centre column by a Zulu diversionary force while the main *impi* attacked his camp. Chelmsford's decision not to set up the British camp defensively, contrary to established doctrine, and ignoring information that the Zulus were close at hand were decisions that the British were soon to regret. The ensuing Battle of Isandhlwana was the greatest victory that the Zulu kingdom would enjoy during the war. The camp of British centre column was annihilated and of all its supplies,ammunition and transport were lost. The defeat left Chelmsford no choice but to hastily retreat out of Zululand. In the battle's aftermath, a party of some 4,000 Zulu reserves mounted an unauthorised raid on the nearby British army border post of Rorke's Drift and were driven off after ten hours of ferocious fighting which gave the British a much needed victory to offset the terrible news of the disaster at Isandhlwana.

While the British central column under Chelmsford's command was thus engaged, the right flank column on the coast, under Colonel Charles Pearson, crossed the Tugela River, skirmished with a Zulu *impi* that was attempting to set up an ambush at the Inyezane River, and advanced as far as the deserted missionary station of Eshowe, which he set about fortifying. On learning of the disaster at Isandhlwana, Pearson made plans to withdraw back beyond the Tugeala River. However, before he had decided whether or not to put these plans into effect, the Zulu army managed to cut off his supply lines, and the Siege of Eshowe had begun.

Meanwhile the left flank column at Utrecht, under Colonel Evelyn Wood, had originally been charged with occupying the Zulu tribes of north-west Zululand and preventing them from interfering with the British central column's advance on Ulundi. To this end Wood set up camp at Tinta's Kraal, just 10 miles south of Hlobane Mountain, where a force of 4,000 Zulus had been spotted. He planned to attack them on 24th January, but on learning of the disaster at Isandhlwana, he decided to withdraw back to the Kraal. Thus one month after the British invasion, only their left flank column remained militarily effective, and it was too weak to conduct a campaign alone. The first invasion of Zululand had been a failure.

It had never been Cetshwayo's intention to invade Natal, but to simply fight within the boundaries of the Zulu kingdom. Safe from the threat of enemy action Chelmsford used the next two months to regroup and build a fresh invading force with the initial intention of relieving Pearson at Eshowe. The British government rushed seven regiments of reinforcements to Natal, along with two artillery batteries.

On 12th March, an armed escort of stores marching to Luneberg, was defeated by about 500 Zulus at the Battle of Intombe; the British force suffered 80 killed and all the stores were lost. The first British reinforcements troops arrived at Durban on 7th March. On the 29th March a British column, consisting of 3,400 British and 2,300 African soldiers, under Lord Chelmsford, marched to the relief of Eshowe, with the lessons of Isandhlwana still fresh in their minds they formed entrenched camps every night.

Chelmsford ordered Sir Evelyn Wood's troops to attack the abaQulusi Zulu stronghold in Hlobane. Lieutenant Colonel Redvers Buller, led the attack on Hlobane on 28th March. However, as the Zulu main army of 20,000 men approached to help their besieged comrades, the British force began a retreat which turned into a rout and were pursued by 1,000 Zulus of the abaQulusi who inflicted some 225 casualties on the British force.

The next day 20,000 Zulu warriors attacked Wood's 2,068 men in a well-fortified camp at Kambula, apparently without Cetshwayo's permission. The British held them off in the Battle of Kambula and after five hours of heavy attacks the Zulus withdrew with heavy losses but were pursued by British mounted troops, who killed many more fleeing and wounded warriors. British losses amounted to 83 (28 killed and 55 wounded), while the Zulus lost up to 2,000 killed. The effect of the battle of Kambula on the Zulu army was severe. Their commander Mnyamana tried to get the regiments to return to Ulundi but many demoralised warriors simply went home.

While Woods was thus engaged, Chelmsford's column was marching on Eshowe. On 2nd April this force was attacked en route at Gingindlovu, the Zulu being repulsed. Their losses were heavy, estimated at 1,200 while the British only suffered two dead and 52 wounded. The next day they relieved Pearson's men. They evacuated Eshowe on 5th April, after which the Zulu forces burned it down.

The new start of the larger, heavily reinforced second invasion was not promising for the British. Despite their successes at Kambula, Gingindlovu and Eshowe, they were right back where they had started from at the beginning of January. Nevertheless, Chelmsford had a pressing reason to proceed with haste – he knew that Sir Garnet Wolseley was being sent to replace him, and he wanted to inflict a decisive defeat on Cetshwayo's forces before then. With yet more reinforcements arriving, the British forces reached a total of 16,000 British and 7,000 Native troops. Chelmsford reorganised his forces and again advanced into Zululand in June, this time with the added precaution building fortified camps all along the way.

One of the early British casualties on the final phase of the war was the exiled heir to the French throne, Imperial Prince Napoleon Eugene, who had volunteered to serve in the British army and was killed on 1st June 1879 while out with a party on reconnaissance .

Cetshwayo, knowing that the newly reinforced British would be a formidable opponent, attempted to negotiate a peace treaty. Chelmsford was not open to negotiations, as he wished to restore his tarnished reputation before Wolseley relieved him of command. With a renewed sense of urgency he proceeded to the final attack on the royal kraal of Ulundi. He was intent on subjecting the main Zulu army to a crushing defeat and he possessed the superior weaponry to achieve that feat. On 4th July the armies clashed at the Battle of Ulundi, and Cetshwayo's forces were decisively defeated.

In recognition of his eventual victory Chelmsford received a Knight Grand Cross of Bath, largely because of Ulundi, however, he was severely criticised by the Horse Guards investigation and he would never serve in the field again. Bartle Frere also lost face and was relegated to a minor post in Cape Town. Following the conclusion of the Anglo-Zulu War, Bishop Colenso interceded on behalf of Cetshwayo with the British government and succeeded in getting him released from Robben Island and returned to Zululand in 1883.

Harford was a witness to many of these events and served with Lord Chelmsford's Column, and was therefore close to key actions such as the initial skirmishes of the war, the disaster at Isandhlwana and the defence of Rorke's Drift. In his journal he describes the recovery at Fugitives' Drift of the Queen's Colour of the 1st Battalion, 24th Regiment, claiming that he personally was responsible for finding the standard. Later, on resuming the Adjutancy of the 99th regiment, he took part in the hunt for the Zulu king, Cetshwayo, after the battle of Ulundi. He writes of Cetshwayo's capture and detention, and tells how he came to know the exiled king very well on a personal level when Harford was stationed at Cape Town in 1881.

This journal therefore is an invaluable addition to the literature of the Zulu War.

Shortly after his death in 1937, the manuscript of Colonel Henry Harford's Zulu War Journal was presented to the Durban Museum. It had been sent out to South Africa from England by his daughter, presumably in accordance with his wishes, and became one of the most treasured possessions of the Old Durban Room collection which was the nucleus of Durban's present-day Local History Museum.

Harford's manuscript is written in black ink in a notebook with soft covers and ruled pages, and the handwriting is neat and clearly legible. The front cover of the book bears an attractive design of shield and assegais drawn and painted by the author and the back cover has also been decorated, though not in colour.

Although the manuscript is undated it is assumed that Harford wrote an account of his Zulu War experiences during or just after the campaign of 1879, and that he copied the narrative into the notebook now in the possession of the Museum many years later, possibly about 1920. It is thought that he made certain additions and revisions during the later copying. Nontheless, the work very much retains the character of a young man's description of, and commentary on, events as they happened.

One of the most important features of Harford's notebook are the small but beautifully-executed pencil sketches made while he was on active service and pasted into the book at appropriate places in the text. Unfortunately these illustrations have now faded with time and unfortunately are no longer capable of adequate reproduction. For the purpose of this edition these sketches, have been replaced by contemporary photographs and illustrations drawn from *The Illustrated London News* and *The Graphic*. Harford himself contributed sketches to *The Illustrated London News* and these vivid depictions add interest of the Journal as a contemporary historical record.

Colonel Henry Charles Harford C.B., was a member of the distinguished English family which is listed in Burke's Landed Gentry as Harford of Horton. Harford's father was Captain Charles Joseph Harford, a retired British Army officer who had served in the 12th Lancers. In 1864, the retired captain bought an estate which he named Stapleton Grove, it was situated at Pinetown, twelve miles inland from Durban. Charles Joseph became a successful tobacco farmer, and was elected as a Member for Durban County in Natal's Legislative Council, a capacity in which he served from 1866 until 1871.

Henry Charles Harford was the only son of Captain Charles Joseph Harford, he was born in 1852 and emigrated to South Africa with his family from England in 1864, he was then aged twelve, and was accompanied by his parents and five young sisters.

Harford Jr. had begun his education at Stoke Grammar School in Plymouth, but he completed it in South Africa, probably in Pieter-maritzburg. He may also have been a private pupil of Canon Gray, who was tutor to Robert and Frank Colenso, sons of the Bishop of Natal who later secured the release of the Zulu king.

Henry Charles Harford appears to have enjoyed an idyllic boyhood. The Natal countryside, both in the Pinetown area and on the North Coast where he spent his holidays, was then wild and unspoilt. As an active young man he plunged into the colonial way of life. He learned to ride and shoot and to camp out and 'do everything for oneself', as he put it. He became an enthusiastic naturalist and was soon recognised as an authority on the birds, butterflies and moths of Natal, crucially he also acquired a fluency in the Zulu language which was to serve him well during the Zulu War of 1879.

Harford Jr. became a close companion of the Colenso boys, as is evidenced by a letter written by their mother to a Mrs. Lyell on July 17th, 1869; Mrs. Colenso wrote that Robert and Frank (who had recently left for England) had had 'just a few friends amongst the selectest of the young military, and one youth who had a passion for natural history, son of a Captain Harford, who lives in the country. Excursions to the mountain for the sake of collecting birds and insects seemed latterly the great object of life…'

The Harford family circle began to break up in 1870, when the eldest daughter, Emma Florence Mary, married Major David Erskine, Colonial Secretary of Natal. A further significant event took place later that year when Harford Jr. sailed for England, with the object of entering the British Army. In the absence of his son Harford Snr. decided to branch out and try his luck at the Kimberley Diamond Fields. Mrs. Harford did not join him and she returned to England with her younger daughters. Unfortunately things did not work out as planned and Captain Harford died in Kimberley in 1874.

In the meantime Henry Harford was accepted as an ensign in the 99th Foot (Duke of Edinburgh's Regiment). He became Adjutant of the regiment in 1877, but resigned from the position towards the end of 1878, when it was apparent that war with the Zulu was imminent, and applied for secondment to the British forces in Natal. His knowledge of the Zulu language gave him an advantage over other candidates, and he was posted immediately to South Africa and on arrival was made Staff Officer to Commandant Lonsdale of the 3rd Regiment, Natal Native Contingent.

Harford resumed the Adjutancy of the 99th (which by then had been sent out to Zululand), in July or August, 1879, and held this post until 1882. In 1898 he took command of the 2nd Battalion, with the rank of Colonel, and was married that year to Miss Florence Page, daughter of Dr. W. Page of the Indian Civil Service. His wife died in 1900, leaving him with a baby daughter named Violet Eva. Harford commanded the 1st Battalion of the 99th Regiment from 1899 to 1902, and England's 62nd Regimental District from 1902 to 1905. From 1905 to 1907 he was Colonel in Charge of Records for the Yorkshire Grouped Regimental Districts. He was awarded the decoration Commander of the Bath in 1907, and after his retirement made his home in Sussex. He died on March 25th, 1937.

Henry Harford had never lost his interest in zoology and entomology (an interest he had acquired as a boy from his father, who was a keen naturalist), and throughout his army career he was constantly adding to his knowledge of animals and insects. As a result the Durban Museum possesses many cases of butterflies, moths and other insects collected and preserved by Harford in India, Malta and other parts of the world where his regiment was stationed.

Bob Carruthers

CHAPTER 1

PREPARATIONS FOR WAR

IN 1878 WE, i.e. the 99th (Duke of Edinburgh's) Regiment were stationed at Chatham whither we had arrived from Templemore. Ireland, in 1877. I had been Adjutant for just a year, when disturbances broke out in Zululand which ended in declaration of war against Cetewayo and the Zulu nation. Officers for special service, as well as troops, were being despatched from Home; and as I had spent the most of my youth, seven years, in Natal and had a very fair knowledge of the Kaffir language, it occurred to me that I should stand a very good chance of getting out if I put in an application. It was an opportunity not to be lost, and although I felt some qualms of conscience in deserting the Regiment after having been so recently appointed Adjutant, I saw the Colonel (Colonel Welman) and asked him if he would have any objection to my sending in an application. At the same time I gave him the name of an officer who was willing to act for me, should my application succeed.

Nothing could have been kinder than the manner in which the Colonel acceded to my request, and after discussing the matter with me at some length, and entering into the problem of my future prospects, being of opinion that I would be certain to get a Staff billet after the War, he advised me to resign the Adjutancy. This I did, and my application for special service was forwarded, with very strong recommendations. Lieutenant Davison, the officer whose name I had submitted to act for me, was eventually appointed Adjutant.

Time having been given for my application to reach the War Office, I got a day's leave to run up to London and see the Adjutant-General, Sir Martin Dillon, personally. Arriving at the War Office at 9 a.m., I was the only solitary individual in the waiting-room till 10 o'clock, when I saw the Adjutant-General go into his office. A few minutes later, I gave the porter my card to hand in as soon as the Adjutant-General was disengaged, but unfortunately did not give him a tip as I ought to have done. Officers of all grades, from Generals to subalterns, belonging to all arms of the Service, now began to pour in, and by 11 o'clock the waiting-room was simply crammed. There was scarcely standing room.

Presently the Adjutant-General began to receive the callers, and instead of my being ushered in as I had fondly hoped, having been the first to arrive, some of the senior officers were called upon. Possibly, of course, they might have attended by appointment. However, shortly before twelve noon Sir Garnet Wolseley arrived, followed by the Duke of Connaught, and until they had taken their departure no further interviews could take place. One o'clock, two o'clock struck, and still there was no sign of their moving, so a good many of those who were waiting, went off. It was not until four o'clock that the Adjutant-General again became available for interviews.

At six o'clock I again found myself the solitary occupant of the waiting-room, so I walked out into the passage, and seeing the porter sitting outside the Adjutant-General's room, said to him, in a fairly loud tone of voice, "Did you present my card to the Adjutant-General this morning? I gave it to you at nine o'clock, and asked you to give it in as soon as he was disengaged; and here I have been waiting ever since." The man then went into the Adjutant-General's room, and I was ushered in at once.

That my conversation with the porter had been overheard was very certain, for Sir Martin Dillon at once said, "I'm so sorry to think that you should have been kept waiting so long", and then added, "Now what can I do for you?" After I had explained my reason for coming, he said, "Sit down at my table, and I will dictate a letter for you." This letter was, of course, to himself, which he there and then countersigned, passed in through a little window to an official in the next room, and gave orders for it to be attended to at once. He then questioned me about Natal, and asked me when I would be prepared to start. "Tomorrow morning, Sir", I said ,'I'm going back to Chatham tonight." "Very well", he said, "The day after tomorrow, you will get your orders", and bade me "Good night." So, after all, my long wait had been a blessing in disguise; and I left the War Office in a true state of delight at my luck.

Having received my orders, as promised by the Adjutant-General, which gave me three days' grace before sailing, I went up to London to do my shopping, going straight to Messrs Silver & Co., 67 Cornhill, where I got everything I required, except boots. While making my purchases I noticed a gentleman following me up very closely, and presently he asked me if I was going to South Africa, as 1 seemed to be selecting the very things suitable for a campaign. He said that he also was going out, and as he was at a loss to know what was best to take, would I allow him to accompany me and make similar purchases? So I gave him my list of things, to copy. He (Lieutenant Courtnay of the 21st Hussars) and I subsequently went out together in the *Edinburgh Castle*.

After Silver's I went to Dean's, in the Strand, for a couple of pairs of porpoise-hide boots, the most essential of all my purchases. Only one of all his ready-made pairs fitted me; and, of course, there was no time to have another pair made. While looking round the shop, however, I saw a pair cut quite differently from any other, stowed away in a corner by themselves. So I said, "Mr Dean, what are these?" "Oh", he said, "They have been made specially to order by a gentleman going out to shoot in Algeria; the front parts have been lengthened so as to form a knee-cap, to avoid the knees being pricked in going through gorse, etc." "Well", I said, "If they fit me, would you let me have them?" I was given them to try on, and they fitted me like a glove. So I got my two pairs, and departed. Of this particular pair of boots I shall later on have an interesting story to relate.

Neville, one of our fellows, met me and we lunched together, after which I took the first train to Bristol, to say "Goodbye" to my grandfather and grandmother at Stapleton, returning to Chatham early the next day. The dear old gentleman gave me £100 as he lay in his bed, and I took my last farewell of him at an early hour in the morning. It was our last meeting, for he passed away some few months later, at a ripe old age.

On the day fixed for sailing, I railed with all my goods and chattels from Chatham to Victoria Station from whence I made out from the time-tables I should get an early train to Dartmouth, where the *Edinburgh Castle* was lying and due to sail at 4 p.m. Arriving full early at the station, I had the baggage weighed and labelled and placed in a heap on the platform convenient for loading up in the van when the train came in. After strolling up and down for about an hour, a porter appeared, and having had a look at the baggage said, "Is this your baggage, Sir?" I said, "Yes". "I see it's labelled for Dartmouth", he said, "You will never get to Dartmouth from here; you ought to have gone to Paddington!" "Good Heavens!" I said, "What on earth is to be done; I must get to Dartmouth by four o'clock today." Then taking out his watch, he said, "There's a direct train leaving Paddington in a quarter of an hour. You may catch it if you look sharp." Whereupon I said, "I'll give you a half-sovereign and pay double fare for a cart, if you can manage it for me."

In an instant, he hailed a drayman with a two-horsed van in the station-yard, who he informed me was a pal of his; and between the two of them my traps were soon in the van. Whilst loading up, the driver was informed that he would get double fare and that "This

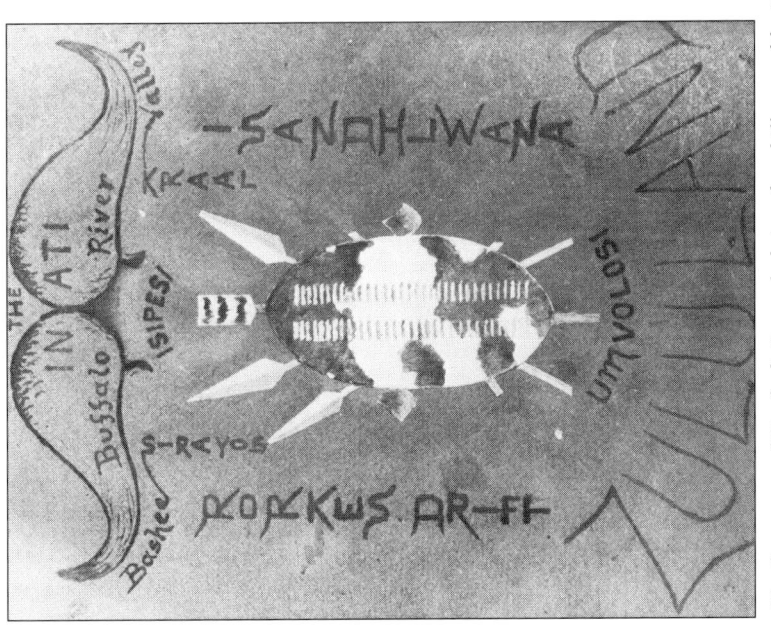

The front cover of Harford's Journal, designed and illustrated by Harford himself is seen here alongside a page from the journal.

gentleman must catch the Dartmouth train leaving Paddington in a quarter of an hour's time!" The porter got his half-sovereign, and I jumped into an hansom cab, following the van. No fire-engine could have gone a better pace than we did, we simply flew through the streets, which, luckily, were pretty empty. At Paddington, happily, there were plenty of porters, and my things, having been already labelled, were soon whipped off. Having paid the driver, I tore off to the ticket-office, and eventually jumped into the train just as it was moving off, the last of my packages being shovelled in while the train was on the move. It was a narrow squeak. As I journeyed along I felt deeply grateful to Providence for coming to my rescue, through the agency of a porter.

On arriving at Dartmouth, I found that the time for sailing had been postponed to midnight; and that a special late train was being run from Paddington for the convenience of passengers to meet this change; so that, really, I need not have hurried as I did. Nevertheless, I had done the right thing, as my baggage was stowed away on board by daylight, and I comfortably settled down in my cabin, whereas the latecomers were wandering about half the night, looking after their belongings.

In the morning I found that Smith-Dorrien, who was in after years to become such a distinguished soldier, was my cabin companion; and I often call to mind his first remark to me, as we met on deck, "I don't know whether I ought to touch my cap to you, or you to me." Anyhow, he was an excellent fellow, and we formed a lasting friendship.

The other officers on board were Cochrane, of the 32nd Regiment, whom I had known in Natal; Courtnay, of the 21st Hussars, my casual shopping acquaintance; Bailey and Mitchell, of the 57th Regiment; Williams, of the 27th Regiment, all Lieutenants, and Captain Sprate, of the 14th Regiment. Needless to say, we soon got to know each other, and spent most of our time in endeavouring to learn signalling. Of course there were many civilian passengers on board, and altogether we had a very pleasant time. The Captain was one of the very best, and was a great favourite with everyone. Cochrane was simply the life and soul of the ship, always ready to sit down at the piano and sing a good song, or get up concerts, theatricals and other amusements. Scarcely a day went by without something going on under his direction. For the concerts and theatricals a small charge was made, and at the end of the voyage I think it was a little over £60 that was handed to the Captain for charitable purposes.

We touched at no Ports till reaching Cape Town, but had a sight of the Canary Islands, Madeira and Ascension. When off Cape Verde, about 150 miles out at sea, I caught a number of little butterflies, "Blues" of the family Lycaenidae, and a few wasps. The former simply swarmed at the stern of the vessel, fascinated, apparently, by the churning up of the water by the propeller. It was a lovely day, and very calm. Notwithstanding the great distance that they had flown out from the shore their flight was still very strong, and they preferred to keep on the wing to settling anywhere on the vessel. Whither their instinct was leading them, it is impossible to say; but I am afraid they were doomed eventually to perish in the ocean.

At Cape Town, everyone on board, I think, took a run ashore. Sissy was then living at Kalk Bay, a watering-place between Cape Town and Simonstown, so I went down to see her; and a more wretched, bare, bleak and uncomfortable-looking place than she was in, it would be almost impossible to find. I then went back to Cape Town to call on Sir Charles Mills and had a long talk with him. The Major was still away somewhere in the Transvaal, getting rid of the £2,500 entrusted to him by Mr. Cleland for the purpose of ostrich-farming. Sir Charles Mills pointed out to me the necessity for both the Major and Sissy returning to England as soon as possible, especially as Sissy had been very ill. It was only a matter of finding the money to pay their passages. He said that he would be perfectly willing to pay for the Major, if I would pay for Sissy. So, as Grandfather had given me £100, I handed over £60 for her passage, thankful to think that I was able to do it.

On our way up the Coast, we stopped at Port Elizabeth only to land one or two passengers. While hanging about outside the harbour, another steamer from England passed, conveying a number of Staff College officers to Natal for special services. We at once dubbed them aasvogels as we were afraid that, on reaching Natal before us, they would be selected for the best appointments; and as the vessel was close enough for visual signalling, we tried our skill with the flags. But nobody took the trouble to communicate with us in return.

On arrival at Durban after a most delightful voyage, we at once scattered. Some of the fellows went straight off to Maritzburg; others remained for a day or two in Durban, to look after their baggage and to obtain their orders from the G.O.C.. Knowing the ins and outs of the place well myself, I took young Williams, a nice youngster afterwards killed at Hlobane, with me to report our arrival to General Bellairs, the G.O.C. After getting our instructions to proceed to Maritzburg for final orders, I went with him on a round of calls to old friends, winding up by dining with Phyllis and Mrs Payne, with whom I left the collection of insects I had made on the voyage. I asked them to hand them over to the Curator of the then, in embryo, Museum, which contained other collections of mine, but I am sorry to say Phil forgot all about it and they were all lost.

An early start was made the next morning, and Mr Welch's bus, which was still running as of yore, brought us into Maritzburg about 7 p.m. by the old familiar road, viz. Berea, Rooi Koppies, Cowie's Hill, Pinetown, Field's and Botha's Hills, Padley's and Camperdown, everywhere recalling happy reminiscences of shooting and collecting. One longed to get out of the bus and have a look round again with the gun and net.

"Cetewayo".

With as little delay as possible, I reported myself at Headquarters and first of all saw General Clifford. He told me that Lord Chelmsford, who was in the next room, wished to see me, and I was thereupon ushered in. After the usual formalities the General said, "Now I am going to give you a very good billet, which will give you ten shillings a day Staff pay. I'm going to appoint you Staff officer to Commandant Lonsdale who will command the 3rd Regiment, Natal Native Contingent, now being organised at Sand Spruit. You will find him an exceedingly nice fellow, and I hope that you will get on well together." Then, after relating to me some of Lonsdale's adventures in the Gaika-Galeka war asked me to lose no time in joining the Natal Native Contingent. Before saying "Good night", I assured the General that he had nothing to fear in regard to my loyalty to Lonsdale; and that nothing would be left undone by me to further the interests of the 3rd Natal Native Contingent in every way, at the same time expressing my gratitude for the appointment. This was a stroke of luck such as I had not counted on; no doubt my being able to speak Zulu had helped me into it.

I put up at the Plough Hotel, which in former days had been the Officers' Mess, and was within a stone's throw of the Major's old house. The members of the Maritzburg Club also very kindly made all of us "Specials" honorary members. When my name appeared in General Orders next day, I was in a position to make final preparations for the Front. I set to work to draw my pony and carbine, which the Government allowed and which, if still in existence at the end of the campaign, had to be returned; visited the Pay Office to present my last pay certificate and get some money: arranged for my baggage to be sent on as soon as it arrived from Durban; got a few items of saddlery from my old friend Williams, the saddler; and, as one pony would not suffice for my work, bought another, a sturdy little grey which afterwards saved the fife of a Corporal of the Contingent, who escaped on it from Isandhlwana, but died from over-exertion in getting over such terrible ground as they traversed.

In a couple of days I was able to start. Riding one pony and leading the other, which carried all my requirements till the wagons arrived at Sand Spruit with the heavier baggage - which was a little over a month - I travelled to Grcytown the first day, about forty-five miles. As there were several nasty crossings and spruits, as well as an uncommonly rough road from there on to Sand Spruit, as well as the distance being a little greater, I stopped the next day at a little wattle-and-daub store, known as Sand Spruit Store, a little more than halfway. This enabled me to get into Camp the following day before it got dark. Luckily, the weather was splendid, otherwise I should have had a bad time of it as after heavy thunderstorms and rain many of the spruits as well as the river crossings arc impassable for a considerable time. Arrived at my journey's end, I found my tent ready pitched for me; and my ponies, which were the first consideration, were soon unsaddled, divested of their traps and taken off to be well groomed and fed. Commandant Lonsdale was away, having gone on a visit to Mr Fynn for ten days, to consult about some Kaffirs as he was magistrate of the Umsinga district and could afford a great deal of assistance.

Large batches of Kaffirs from all parts poured into Camp daily, in charge of their respective indunas, and the work of organisation went on rapidly. The European officers and N.C.O.'s had all arrived, and Lonsdale had already told them off to their Battalions... Commandant Hamilton-Browne, "Maori" Browne, as he was called, had the 1st Battalion and Commandant Cooper ' the 2nd... All were adventurers, and all the very best of fellows, ready to do anything and go anywhere. The strength of each Battalion was laid down to be 1 000 men, but before we crossed into the Zulu country this number had been considerably increased and we found it impossible to get rid of these additional men, as the Government ration of meat proved too attractive.

All natives on the strength were served out with a blanket, and a red cloth headband as a distinguishing mark. A hundred in each battalion were armed with rifles and the remainder with billhooks, but undoubtedly they put much more faith in their own assegais and shields. Drilling went on throughout the day, and kept everyone hard at work. By the time Lonsdale returned everything was in working order and discipline and drill were the main points to be attended to. Our camp lay at the foot of the high range of hills at Helpmekaar, on the Rorke's Drift road, and a more stony or rocky position could not well have been selected. On several occasions we were nearly washed away during heavy thunderstorms, owing to the tentpegs not holding, while lighting fires for meals was out of the question.

It was a day or two before one of these terrific storms that Norris-Newman, the Special Correspondent for the London Standard and Cape Standard and Mail arrived, accompanied by our Medical Officer, Dr Bercsford, about a week before Christmas, and quietly plumped himself down on us, and without any by or with your leave announced his intention of attaching himself to the Contingent. This was quite an unlooked-for surprise, more especially as none of us had ever seen or heard of him before. Nevertheless, we made him very welcome, and he turned out to be an excellent and garrulous companion in our Mess. Lonsdale at once dubbed him "Noggs", and by this name he was subsequently known throughout the 3rd Column. At the end of the Campaign he wrote a book entitled, In Zululand With the British Throughout the War of 1879, and in it he describes his first experience of Sand Spruit when he was drowned out of his tent and had to go to bed supperless, an item not at all in keeping with his taste.

Accompanying the Contingent, by permission of the Authorities, as lookers-on or Native Staff, we had two of Cetewayo's brothers,

Umkungu and Isikota, and a witchdoctor named Ingabangi. The two brothers had escaped with their mother from Zululand some time before, at the time of the massacre of Umbelazi and his followers. Isikota was a very fine specimen, and very like his father in features. Ingabangi was rather a wizened-up old man, but an eloquent speaker, and looked upon with great respect by the natives.

The surroundings of my tent were looked upon as the "Indaba" ground; and all who had complaints to make, or who wished to ask questions, found their way there early in the morning, and squatted patiently and silently in rows or semicircles until I made my appearance. It need hardly be said that the chief topic of conversation was grub, and especially as to who were going to get the heads of the cattle killed for consumption that particular day. One morning I had a really wonderful, and at the same time very pleasant, surprise sprung on me. During the indaba a man suddenly stood up in the middle of the assembly and, putting his hand to his chin, exclaimed, "Waugh! Ow!! Warn Charlie!!!" So I called him up and found that he had worked on our farm at Pinetown. More than eight years had passed since he had last seen or heard of me, and I might have been in Kamchatka for all he knew. Although, perhaps, as a young man I had not changed very much in features, yet under the circumstances the quickness with which he recognised me showed the retentive memory and powers of observation that he possessed. I took him on at once as my personal servant, and stuck to his old name of "Jim". More will be said of him later on.

It was now nearing the 11th January, the date fixed for the troops to move across the border. Lord Chelmsford had arrived at Rorke's Drift and Lonsdale rode over to have an interview with him but received no definite orders with regard to the movements of the Contingent. However, one morning I had occasion to go to Rorke's Drift myself, to see the Adjutant-General, Major Clery,

Members of the Natal Native Contingent armed with assegais and shields, c1879.

(afterwards, General Sir Francis Clery). Luckily, arriving at a very early hour, and having completed my work with him, I was on the point of mounting my pony to ride back to camp, when Major Clery said, "You will have everything ready, Harford, won't you, for the General today?" "Good Heavens, Major", I said, "This is the first I've heard about his coming!" "You don't mean to say that Lonsdale never told you about it?", he replied, "He is going to inspect you at twelve o'clock. The General gave Lonsdale his orders days ago."

Well, I rode off as hard as I could go, to Camp. I found Lonsdale sitting in his tent, looking over his Masonic orders and paraphernalia, and, on my breaking the news to him as quickly as I could, he said, "Good God! I forgot all about it. Shout for my pony, like a good chap."

I also got a change of ponies. Kaffirs were sent out in all directions to call in the men who were drilling, many of them miles away. As soon as the ponies were ready, we jumped on, Lonsdale saying, "You take that way; I'll take this", and we went off at a gallop. We had scarcely parted company when Lonsdale's pony shied at something and threw him off. I saw the fall. He appeared to have struck his head and then, rolling over on his back, lay quite still with one of his arms projecting in the air at right angles to his body. I got off at once and ran to his assistance, only to find that he was unconscious, and rigidly stiff. I shouted for the Doctor, and as soon as he had come up with some Natives and a stretcher, I galloped off again to collect the men. Eventually, after a real race for it, everybody was got in; but Hamilton-Browne and Cooper were still getting their Battalions formed up on parade when the General and staff made their appearance.

I had, of course, to ride out and tell the General what had happened. So we first went to Lonsdale's tent, and finding that he was still unconscious, orders were given for his removal to Helpmekaar hospital. It was found afterwards that he had received concussion of the brain. (He rejoined the Contingent the day we went into camp at Isandhlwana, being received with a loud "*Bayete*". Through his interpreter, he expressed his pleasure at what he had seen, and gave some sound advice on matters of discipline, especially behaviour towards women and children and prisoners.)

On the following day we moved to Rorke's Drift, where Major Black, of the 2nd Battalion, 24th Regiment was given temporary command until Lonsdale returned. Before crossing into Zululand, the Battalion Commanders devised an excellent plan for keeping their various Companies intact, and for recognising them in the field should they become separated or lose themselves, viz: by having small flags made with the number of the Battalion, 1 or 2, and some special device for each Company painted on them. These devices represented, as nearly as possible, the soubriquets the Natives had imposed upon themselves, such as the *ingulube* (pigs), *izinkunzana* (young bulls), and so forth. This caused great delight, and gave rise to endless chaff and amusement on all occasions.

When the general advance took place, a few of our Natives under a corporal named Schiess were left at Rorke's Drift as part of the Garrison of the Fort under Lieutenant Bromhead, of the 2nd Battalion, 24th Regiment, and Lieutenant Chard, of the Royal Engineers. Schiess was subsequently awarded the Victoria Cross for very conspicuous bravery. Some of the men of the 24th Regiment told me that he fought like a tiger and at one time, when some Zulus actually managed to clutch hold of his bayonet, he got it out of their hands and, springing over the parapet, bayonetted some six or seven of them straight away.

- CHAPTER 2 -
ISANDHLWANA

On the 11th January the 3rd Column crossed the Buffalo into Zululand, the troops making their way over at different points. The Artillery and the 24th Regiment went over by degrees in the pontoon, a little above the main Drift, known as Rorke's Drift after the Dutchman Jim Rorke, whose house and farm buildings were occupied by us as a Fort, after being entrenched. I was ordered to find a crossing for the 2nd/3rd Natal Native Contingent, higher up the river. The fog was so dense one could barely see anything a yard in front, but at last, after hugging the bank very closely for about half a mile or more, we came to a spot that looked worth a trial. So I put my pony at it and got across all right, the bed of the river being nice and hard; but the water came up to the saddle flaps, and there was a nasty bank to scramble up on the opposite side. However, that did not matter, it was good enough.

Then followed a truly unforgettable scene, first of the Natives crossing over and then of the impressive ceremony when the Regiment had formed up again on the other side and were addressed by old Ingabangi, the witch-doctor. In order to scare away any crocodiles that might be lurking in the vicinity, the leading Company formed a double chain right across the River, leaving a pathway between for the remainder to pass through. The men forming the chain clasped hands, and the moment they entered the water they started to hum a kind of war-chant, which was taken up by every Company as they passed over. The sound that this produced was like a gigantic swarm of bees buzzing about us, and sufficient to scare crocodiles or anything else, away. Altogether, it was both a curious and grand sight.

Soldiers of 24th Regiment of Foot.

All being safely over, the men were formed up in quarter-column on the hillside, and one or two Officers on their ponies were sent out in different directions to try and find out in the dense fog where any of the other troops were, and what was going on. While this was in progress, old Ingabangi asked permission to address the men. Never shall I forget his extraordinary elocutionary power, and the splendid oration he delivered. The old fellow got to the head of the Column and then started off at a trot, going backwards and forwards at this pace for nearly an hour. He would have gone on much longer, had we not received orders to move. Without stopping to take breath, he recounted the history of the Zulu nation, which was frequently applauded by a loud "Gee!" and rattling of assegais on shields from the whole Contingent. It was a wonderfully impressive scene, and one which will always remain fresh in my memory. The drift at which we crossed was subsequently known as Harford's Drift, but I don't suppose it has been used since.

Our scouts eventually got in touch with the 24th Regiment, and as we moved up to support them the fog gradually lifted. Then a very pretty sight presented itself as the troops were dotted about over the rolling hills in "Receive Cavalry" squares formation, their red coats showing up distinctly in the clear atmosphere. No further advance was made that day, owing to the difficulties of getting the Transport across. So we camped where we were.

During the day, Major Dartnell with a few Mounted Police were out on a reconnaissance, and took me with him as Staff Officer. On our way up the Bashee valley towards Sirayo's kraal we heard a war-song being sung, evidently by a large body of Natives; but where they were, or what became of them, we were unable to find out. However, as this was the ground over which we were going to attack the next day, it looked as if it were certain that we should meet with some opposition. Other parties had also been out in various directions, and had captured a considerable number of cattle.

Reveille sounded very early, about 3 a.m. the next morning, and we marched to attack Sirayo's kraal, up the Bashee valley, through thick bush. It was most unpleasant going, for above us, on our right, were hills with the usual cavernous rocks encircling them a little below their crests. It was evident that the warriors we had heard singing their war-chant the day before were ensconced in these caves, for the instant the troops got within range a continuous popping went on from these places. The crack, crack, crack of their guns and rifles echoed and re-echoed among the hills in the still morning air and made it impossible to detect exactly where the shots were coming from. Now and again a Zulu was seen in the open, and on one such occasion I saw the man taking deliberate aim at Colonel Glyn who was standing in an open patch above me. Shouting as loud as I could, I told him to get out of the way before the shot was fired.

Colonel Glyn was in command of the troops, and Lord Chelmsford took up a position with his staff on the opposite side of the valley, to watch operations. Colonel Degacher commanded the 2nd Battalion, 24th Regiment, and Major Black our Contingent, as Lonsdale was still in hospital. We started skirmishing through the bush, Major Black leading the 1st Battalion N.N.C. under Commandant Hamilton-Browne, and I following in support with the 2nd Battalion under Commandant Cooper. Before many minutes, bullets were whizzing about in all directions, and one of our Natives, who was close by my side, got a bullet in the thigh, breaking the bone. A short distance further on, seeing two N.C.O.'s sheltering behind a rock instead of leading their men, I went to drive them on; and had just got them away when "ping" came a bullet and cut away a branch just at the spot where my head was a second before. This was luck!

As we got further into the bush all sorts of obstacles, such as rocky ground, ravines, and especially thick masses of creepers, prevented any sort of formation being properly kept, in consequence of which the firing line and supports soon got mingled together. Nevertheless, the men were kept well in hand. Before very long I could hear Major Black's shrill voice in broad Scotch urging his men on, and, making my way up to him with supports, I found that he and Commandant Hamilton-Browne were in a hot corner close to some caves, with hand-to-hand fighting going on. When I was within about twenty or thirty yards of the place, one of their men fell almost at my feet with a terrible assegai wound, which had nearly cut him in half, right down the back. The poor fellow was not dead, and although I could see it was only a matter of minutes my feelings almost led me to try to put him out of his misery with my revolver. But I abstained. I went on to the ridge of the spur of the hill in front of me as fast as I could, with some men, to see what was on the other side and to assist on Major Black's flank.

Officers of the 24th Regiment of Foot.

Eventually, on reaching the foot of a ledge of rocks, where they curved in a horse-shoe bend overhanging a deep valley, a somewhat grim sight presented itself. Confronting me across the bend was a large, open-mouthed cave, apparently capable of holding a good number of men, and hanging below it were several dead Zulus, caught in the monkey-rope creepers and bits of bush. They had evidently been shot and had either fallen out, or been thrown out, by their comrades when killed. Later on, I learned that a Company of the 24th Regiment had been firing at this particular cave for some time, and had been ordered to cease firing on it when our men came up. It was an uncommonly awkward place to get at, as it meant climbing over nothing but huge rocks and in many places having to work one's way like a crab, besides which a loss of foothold might have landed one in the valley below. However, there was not much time to think, and I determined to make an attempt, so, sending some men to work round below, I took a European N.C.O. who was close at hand, and told him to follow me. Clambering at once over a big piece of rock, I got rather a rude shock on finding a Zulu sitting in a squatting position behind another rock, almost at my elbow. His head showed above the rock, and his wide-open eyes glared at me; but I soon discovered that he was dead.

Scarcely had I left this apparition behind than a live Zulu… suddenly jumped up from his hiding place and, putting the muzzle of his rifle within a couple of feet of my face, pulled the trigger. But the cap snapped, whereupon he dropped his rifle and made off over the rocks for the cave, as hard as he could go. Providence had again come to my aid, and away I went after him, emptying my revolver at him as we scrambled up. Out of my six shots only one hit him, but not mortally. I stopped for a second to reload, but finding the wretched thing stuck I threw it down into the valley below, at the same time turning round and shouting to the N.C.O., who I thought was following me, to let me have his revolver. But he remained behind, where I had left him at the start, and all he did was to call out, as loud as he could, "Captain Harford is killed!" However, I soon put this right by shouting down, "No, he is not, he is very much alive!"

All this was a matter of seconds, and after pronouncing my blessings pretty freely on the Corporal, followed up my quarry, who by this time was standing in the mouth of the cave. Speaking to him in Kaffir, I called upon him to surrender, explaining that I had no intention to harm him in any way and would see to it that he was not ill-treated by anyone. He then squatted down in submission. Before getting up into the cave myself, not caring to run my head into a noose thoughtlessly, I demanded to know if there was anyone else inside and was assured that there was no-one, and as all was quiet, although I must say I had some slight misgivings, I clambered in.

Close to the entrance lay a wounded man with his feet towards me. Although unable to rise, he clutched hold of an assegai that was by his side, but I told him at once to drop it, that I was going to do him no harm, and questioned him as to who was with him in the cave. He stoutly denied that there were any others there. By this time I was getting accustomed to the darkness, and saw several likely-looking boltholes and kept on repeating that I knew there were others somewhere in hiding and that they were telling me lies. At the same time adding, in a tone loud enough to be heard by anyone near the place, that if they would come out I would promise on oath that no harm should be done to them and that I would accompany them myself to the General... who would see that they were well treated.

In a short time this had the desired effect, and presently a head appeared from a hole, and as the object crept out I kept careful watch for any sort of weapon that might emerge with it; another and then another crawled out from the same spot. All were unarmed, and squatted down close to me. I then wanted to know where the others

Isandhlwana: the dash with the colours.

were, but they swore that there was no-one else. As this seemed to be the case, I moved off with my four prisoners, leaving the badly-wounded man in the cave. We soon made out way down the valley to where the General and his staff were, and I was met by Major Clery, the Adjutant-General, who greeted me with, "Well, Harford, I congratulate you on your capture, the General and I have been watching your gallantry for some time." Then he told me that a section of the 24th Regiment had been firing into the cave half the morning, owing to the sniping that had been going on from it, and when Lonsdale's men were seen to be approaching, orders had been sent to them to cease fire. Having handed over my prisoners and telling the Adjutant-General the promise I had made them, and after seeing the man that I had myself wounded was placed in the ambulance wagon for conveyance to hospital, I went off again.

On getting back to the Contingent, one of the men walked up to me and with the usual salutation of "Inkosi" gravely handed me my sword, spurs and courier bag, all of which had been torn off me in walking through the bush, as well as the discarded revolver. Never was I more thankful than to get these things back, especially the courier bag which had been a parting gift from my Captain, Captain Moir, when I left Chatham and contained my field glasses, knife, fork and spoon, as well as other valuable odds and ends. It would have been almost impossible to have found them again, even if a search party had been sent out, but luckily this Good Samaritan had followed carefully in my tracks and picked up the things as they were dropped. Curious to say, in the excitement of the moment I never felt anything going.

Now that the Cavalry, Mounted Police and 24th Regiment had gone on to Sirayo's kraal, one or two companies of the Contingent were sent off to capture some cattle, and after a short rest and a meal the whole force returned to camp, drenched to the skin in a thunderstorm. After a day's rest to clean arms and dry clothing, camp was moved forward to the Bashee Valley, not far from the scene of our operations two days before, and here we remained for the next four or five days, the 24th and ourselves working hard at making and repairing roads for our advance to Isandhlwana on the 20th.

In the meantime representatives from all the units of the Force went out with Major Clery... to select positions within the encampment... At the conclusion of our work we... saw a remarkable instance of how a Pauw - the African Bustard - will squat if he has been unobserved or thinks so. Having ridden all over the ground to be occupied... Major Clery drew rein and we all, some eight or ten of us, formed up in a semicircle round him to receive his final orders. While he was talking I spotted a Pauw lying as flat as he could make himself, with his head stretched straight on the ground like a snake, just between his horse and mine, almost being trodden upon, and called attention to it. Everyone of course took a quid peep at it, and when the Adjutant-General had finished his discourse we rode gently away without disturbing it. For a considerable time afterwards we rode about the ground and kept an eye on the spot, but the bird never stirred while we were there.

Commandant Lonsdale rejoined us before the move to Isandhlwana, quite recovered from his accident, and Monday, the 20th January, saw us on the road to that now historic campaign ground, and a stiff day's work it was, large working-parties both from the 24th and ourselves having to be sent forward to render the road passable for the wagons. If it hadn't been for the services of two of our officers, Captain Kron and Lieutenant Vane, who were expert wagon-drivers and did nearly the whole of the driving themselves at the bad places, many would have broken down and the Column would have been delayed for weeks. As it was, we got in in time to get the tents pitched during the afternoon. Our camp was on the extreme left, close to the main road and just below Isandhlwana hill itself, with our wagons parked at the base of it immediately in our rear. Plenty of wood being close at hand behind the hill, the Natives soon set to work to run up shelters for themselves on the other side of the road, clear of our camp. A queer-looking place they made of it, being packed like sardines, the space allotted to them being limited.

Late in the evening Lonsdale was sent for by the General. I was sitting in Pope's tent (one of the young fellows of the 24th Regiment) at the time, looking at some of his sketches and he at mine, and presently he came to tell me that the 3rd N.N.C. were to start at daybreak the next morning and reconnoitre the ground over the Malakata Hills, together with some Mounted Police under Major Dartnell, who were to work round on our left. Two companies of the Contingent from each Battalion were to be left in camp to furnish outposts and a camp guard, and food taken out for the day. Very stupidly, however, very few of us took out anything but a few biscuits, thinking that we should be back in camp again before nightfall, but our experience on this occasion taught us a lesson that I don't suppose any of us have forgotten, as it was some fifty-six hours, or a little over two days, before we got any more food of any sort, though there was splendid water to drink everywhere. As soon as Lonsdale had given me his instructions, the necessary orders were issued and I went off to see the officers of the four companies detailed to remain in Camp, as all for outpost duty would have to parade at once and accompany me to their positions.

One or two of them were terribly disappointed at the thought of being left behind in Camp and lose the chance of a fight, and begged hard to be allowed to find substitutes, and as these were forthcoming, matters were satisfactorily arranged. Little did any of us conjecture what a momentous difference these exchanges were going to make in the course of some twenty-four hours, and many messages have I received since the campaign ended, and particularly from a Lieutenant Thompson, who now lives in London (having married a very rich wife), declaring that I saved their lives.

Battle of Isandhlwana (1879). Painting by Charles Edwin Fripp (1854-1906).

To any who watched our departure as dawn broke we must have afforded some considerable amusement going off as we did like a swarm of bees in a sort of "Devil take the hinder-most" fashion. The Natives, who had been cooking and eating most of the night, still had pots full of smoking hot porridge which they brought on to parade with them, determined to leave nothing in the shape of food behind, and as it would never have done to take any notice of this irregularity we let them travel at their own pace and get well ahead so as to snatch time to finish their meal. A real cheery lot they all were - full of buoyant spirits and chaff, excellent fellows to work with… but, as was found out too late in the campaign, quite useless as fighters.

As the sun rose that morning there was a very wonderful sky scene. Overhanging Isandhlwana and the camps was a long, tortuous, more or less low-lying dark cloud, based on the horizon, much in the same form as a trail of smoke from the funnel of a steamer and ending immediately above Isandhlwana hill, which as the sun got higher was first tinted almost blood red, then passing into ashy-brown with broad golden edges, assumed a marvellous variety of tints with the rise of the sun. And there it hung for the best part of the morning, frowning, as it were, over the fated Camp. I have never forgotten it. After several hours we arrived at a beautiful spot where a stream that ran through the valley above us dropped over a precipice in a most picturesque waterfall, and on getting up into the valley, which was a dense mass of mimosa bush with precipitous krantzes and kloofs on either side, and Zulu kraals and mealie fields dotted about down below, the Battalions separated, Lonsdale with the 1st Battalion, 3rd N.N.C. taking the left of the stream and I with the 2nd Battalion the right. As we worked our way along, the 1st Battalion managed to capture a considerable number of cattle, but we saw none. All the kraals that we came across were empty, and no Zulus were seen by anyone.

About midday a halt was made for a frugal meal and a rest, as most of us, and especially the Europeans who were on foot, were very nearly dead beat. At the head of the valley the two Battalions got together again, somewhere between 4 and 5 p.m. and went on to the Isipezi hill, Lonsdale riding off to see Major Dartnell, who was with the Mounted Police a mile or so to our left.

The sun was full setting as we reached the top of the Isipezi, and as we got to the ridge the Natives, with their sharp eyes, at once spotted a lot of Zulus on the opposite hill, across a very steep and rugged valley about 800 or 900 yards off in a straight line. The men were ordered to keep well out of sight below the hill, and from behind some rocks Hamilton-Browne, Cooper and I watched the Zulus stealthily moving about, their outline being well defined against the clear evening sky. Before long Major Dartnell joined us with his mounted men; they also had seen the enemy and had found them to be occupying a very strong position, and as it was still daylight he called for volunteers to go over and try to draw the Zulus out in order to see what sort of force confronted us.

Instantly a number of men jumped on their horses and were off, with orders on no account to engage the enemy but simply draw him out and then gallop back. The manoeuvre was most successful; scarcely had our men crossed the valley and got up to within some 800 yards of their position than a regular swarm of Zulus, that we estimated to be over 1 000 men, swept down upon them in their horn formation and tried to surround them. Our men got back as hard as they could; no shots were fired and the Zulus returned back over their hill again. A council of war was now held, and Major Dartnell decided that the troops should bivouac on the spot, a message being sent to the General at once by Lieutenant Walsh (Somerset Light Infantry), with his three mounted infantrymen to explain our position and asking for reinforcements and food. It was very evident that we were opposite a very large *impi*, if not the whole Zulu army.

Walsh's was a very perilous journey with a fifteen-mile ride in the dark over very stiff country, hills, valleys, bush, krantzes, dongas, etc., all quite unknown to him. An occasional Kaffir path, perhaps, leading to goodness knows where, and with every chance of being attacked by a lurking body of Zulus. However, he managed to reach the camp at Isandhlwana safely, and in time for the reinforcements we asked for reaching us by daybreak the next morning, as on the receipt of Major Dartnell's message the General himself started off without a moment's delay, marching through the night with a squadron of Mounted Infantry, seven companies of the 2nd Battalion, 24th Regiment, and four (seven-pounder) guns under Colonel Harness, R.A.

There was some grumbling among the officers of the Native Contingent, who were tired out, at having to bivouac without food, forage or blankets (the Natives all carried their blankets on their persons), and two young officers, Lieutenants Avery and Holcroft, went off without leave, evidently to ride back to camp, but were never seen or heard of again. We bivouacked that night in a hollow square, the Contingent forming the front, right and rear faces, two-company deep and the mounted men on the left. Where the mounted men tethered their horses I don't know, but our animals were all ringed together in a clump in the centre with saddles off, except mine as I should have to be constantly on the move all night while Lonsdale was superintending the formation of the bivouac. I went off to post the outposts. It was now getting dark, and a rare business it was. The Natives showed unmistakable signs of being in a mortal funk, and all wanted to clump together in one spot. At last, however, we strung them out like a thread of beads, each man squatting and touching his neighbour, and behind each section a European N.C.O. and a superior Native were ordered to keep up a continual patrol to see that they kept awake and didn't stir from their position. The captains and other company officers then exercised further control over their own men. In this manner more than a mile of outposts were strung out, almost encircling the bivouac. By this time the Zulus had lighted fires all along their position and kept them going throughout the night, and from this fact we felt pretty certain that we would be attacked in the morning. There was very little fear of a real attack during the night, as night fighting was not the Zulu method.

Having satisfied myself that the outposts were working, and after taking special note of different features, such as bushes, rocks, etc. to guide me on my visits during the night, I got back to the bivouac. Then, hitching my pony on to the others, went to report to Lonsdale whom I found sitting chatting with some of the officers and "Newman Noggs". I think the subject of this conversation was food, everyone was hungry and from my holster I produced a solitary biscuit that had been husbanded all day, which we all shared, each of us getting a piece about the size of a shilling which was better than nothing.

British Gatling guns, 1879.

Intending to make a round of the outposts again in about an hour's time, I plumped myself down to snatch a rest and a short sleep, but had scarcely closed my eyes when bang went a shot from somewhere in the outpost line, and in a second the whole square rose up. Hearing the noise the men were making, rattling their shields and fumbling about for their things, I rushed up and speaking to them in their own language ordered them to keep quiet and lie down. Their own company officers, too, did all they could to establish calm, but it was of no avail. The whole lot made a clean bolt of it and came bounding over us like frightened animals, making their way down the hillside behind us. In this terrific stampede of some 4 000 men the wretched ponies were swept along in a solid mass, kicking and struggling… with several Europeans hanging on to try and stop them. As these passed me, on looking round I caught a glimpse of both Lonsdale and "Noggs" turning a somersault as a lot of Natives bounded over them. Poor "Noggs", who highly resented such treatment, spent the rest of the night with the Mounted Police, having, as he afterwards told me, "had enough of the Contingent".

Amid all this confusion, someone managed to get my pony free and brought him to me, for which I was more than thankful as the situation was serious and I was now able to go in pursuit of the runaways who, at the pace they were going and the rate at which Kaffirs can travel, might soon be out of reach. Luckily, however, I found them almost at the foot of the hill, squatting in various-sized clumps, and addressing them in anything but Parliamentary language, hounded them back to the bivouac. In the darkness of the night it was impossible to say whether everyone had been rounded up, but there was no time for further search as I had to get out to the outpost line as quickly as I could.

Leaving the company officers to get their men together again, and having learnt that no reports had come in from the outposts, I went off to see what had happened, making as straight as I could for the nearest company on the extreme left of the line. On arriving at the spot where they had been posted, not a soul was to be seen, but only a very short distance from me a dark mass of something that I had no recollection of having seen when posting the men loomed up largely to my front. "Zulus!", I said to myself, and rather a shiver went down my back. Everything was dead silence, and I sat on my pony for some minutes, watching it, but as no movement took place, and feeling certain that I was mistaken, rode up to it and found that it was nothing but a mass of rock cropping out of the ground, which had not caught my eye by daylight but in the darkness showed up considerably. The company, however, had vanished.

Further on, I was more successful and found Lieutenant Thompson with his company intact, and as we met I asked him what on earth had happened at the outpost, and told him all that had taken place at the bivouac. He solved the problem by telling me that an N.C.O. of one of his sections, who should have been patrolling in company with a Native, had sat down and fallen asleep, then suddenly waking up and seeing, as he thought, a Zulu coming towards him, fired at him. He said, "It's no use your going any further, as directly the shot was fired the remainder of the outpost went. There is no-one now on my front."

However, I thought it best to go and see for myself, but only found that he was quite right. Everyone but his company had vanished. A nice state of things, had we been really attacked! By the time I had completed my rounds, dawn had broken, and just as I was getting to the top of the hill near the bivouac I saw the General and his staff coming up below me, so went down to meet them. Numerous questions were asked, as to where the bivouac was, what we had seen of the enemy, etc., and I was able to point out a few Zulus still hanging about on the opposite hill-top, as well as some of their fires which were still smoking. After which I conducted them to where Major Dartnell and Lonsdale were, when plans were thought out.

Heavy mists hung over the tops of all the hills till the sun appeared and cleared the atmosphere, when our Force advanced to attack, supported by the troops the General had brought out with him and which were now in the valley below us. The Contingent were ordered to sweep over the Isilulwane hill, where the Zulus had kept their fires burning during the night, and then work on to Matyana's stronghold a little to the right of it. Not a Zulu was to be seen when we got over the rise, and as we afterwards found out, their fires were only a blind to mislead us as to their intentions, and the few men that we had seen exposing themselves and moving about had only been left there to make us imagine that the place was occupied by a large force. On finding no enemy we swung round, descending the other side of the hill, and crossed the valley on to Matyana's stronghold, a hill with nothing but a mass of huge rocks with numerous caves. Here we met with a rather warm reception, bullets began to rain down upon us from all directions, and a few men were hit. It became quite clear that

'The Battle of Isandhlwana'.
(London Illustrated News)

a systematic attack would have to be made on the position, so the two battalions were closed in and formed up in as sheltered a position as we could find, for the companies to be told off for specific work on the front and flanks. While this being done, both Lonsdale and Hamilton-Browne went off in pursuit of some mounted Zulus, evidently Chiefs, who had been seen somewhere on our right, and we never saw them again till late in the afternoon, when they brought in the news of the terrible disaster that had overtaken the camp at Isandhlwana.

In Lonsdale's absence I sent the companies off on their different ways, and continued to conduct the operations myself. Being day instead of night, our men showed nothing of the fear they had exhibited at the bivouac, and under the leadership of the officers did uncommonly well, tackling several very nasty situations. At one spot alone, thirteen men were shot down one after another, and others were quite game to make further attempts had I not gone up myself and put a stop to an impossible undertaking. Nothing but some high explosive like dynamite could have effected an entrance to the cave, which was evidently cut well into the hillside, and the only way to get into it was by a hole underneath a massive overhanging rock, above rather a deep donga. A widish crack through the rock enabled those inside to fire straight down the donga, and made it certain death to attempt to cross it, and above again an extension of the crack provided another place to fire through, making any attempt to get at anyone inside the cave from there impossible, so 1 ordered the men to leave it alone and get on.

Somebody, however, later on, had a lot of brushwood brought up and thrown into the donga with the idea of smoking the Zulus out, but this was put a stop to. At another place where several of us were being held up by snipers, I spotted a man at the entrance hole of a mass of large rock some twenty or thirty yards off taking a deliberate aim at me, and... I quickly shot at him. I then went after him, and, crawling on all fours, found him badly wounded, with a dead Zulu lying close to him. It was a curious little den, quite lighted up through the aperture in the rocks, with space enough for four or five men, and on one side a natural shelf of flat rock much like a bunk on board ship, broad enough for a man to lie on.

Having got the man out and sent him back to the Doctor, we continued the fight, which went on till about midday when Major Clery rode up and ordered me to take the 3rd N.N.C. back a few miles to the Amange Gorge and let them fall out, as the General had sent into camp for provisions and intended to camp there that night. On reaching Amange, and after warning the men not to get out of reach of bugle call, they were told to fall out, and in less than five minutes there was not a vestige to be seen of something like 4,000 men; being hungry, they bounded off like a herd of scared deer in all directions in search of kraals and mealie fields, and were soon out of sight.

Not very long after the men had dispersed, and somewhere about 2 p.m., the Headquarters' bugle sounded and I at once rode off to where the General and his staff were located, and received orders to get the Contingent together at once and bring them up. This took some little doing, as many of the men were miles off, however we eventually arrived at the general rendezvous. Here, the first person I came across was Major Black, 2nd Battalion, 24th Regiment, who, like other officers, was scanning the ground towards Isandhlwana with his field-glasses and was evidently in a great state of anxiety. I said to him, "What's happening, Major?", and he replied, "The camp has been attacked and something very serious has occurred", adding, as he turned to ride away, in his peculiarly delightful Scotch accent, "E-h, Harford, keep your d… d black fellows well out of the way!"

While our men were being formed up, I proceeded to have a look at Isandhlwana and the camp myself, with my glasses, and could only see two tents standing not far from the "neck", and these looked partially black as scorched by fire, but was unable to see a living creature of any sort.

News now began to leak out, and our movements made more clear. While we were fighting at Matyana's the General had received reports from the mounted men that the camp at Isandhlwana was being attacked, hence the reason for the order for the Contingent to retire to Amange. Then, after our men had all been let loose, further and more serious reports had come in, and finally we were assembled preparatory to an advance on the Camp, when Lonsdale's message to the General, written on a scrap of paper, "For God's sake, come. The camp has been taken", was brought in by Hamilton-Browne.

Both Lonsdale and Hamilton-Browne, as I have already said, left us at Matyana's… and both apparently found their way to the camp at Isandhlwana, but Lonsdale evidently got their first. In a fit of absentmindedness he rode straight into the Camp and, as

'The Field of Isandhlwana Revisited'. This sketch shows General Marshall's first arrival at the scene of the slaughter in May 1879.
(London Illustrated News)

he told me afterwards, got up to where his tent was pitched when he suddenly discovered nothing but Zulus looting and dressed in soldiers' coats, whereupon he turned round and rode away. Apparently the apparition of a live white man in their midst, when they felt certain that they had killed everyone, so alarmed them that they let him go unheeded - a marvellous adventure!!! When well clear, of course he rode for dear life to bring the terrible news to the General, but before he could reach Headquarters his pony, Dot, became exhausted, and by a piece of luck Hamilton-Browne (who on approaching the camp had found his way barred by Zulus and was returning with the news) met him, and as his pony was fairly fresh Lonsdale sent on his chit to the General by him and then came slowly on, leading his pony.

By the time the Scouts and reconnoitring parties who had been recalled, and other units, had assembled at the rendezvous it was nearly four o'clock, and before being formed up for attack the General briefly addressed the troops, telling them that the Camp had been taken and saying that he relied on us to re-take it. We then marched off in the following order:

The four guns, Royal Artillery, in the centre, with companies of the 2nd Battalion, 24th Regiment on either flank. On either side of them again, a little to the rear, our Contingent, Lonsdale with the 1st Battalion, 3rd N.N.C. on the left and myself with the 2nd Battalion on the right. Beyond us again on either flank were the Mounted troops. When getting within about a mile of the camp a large body of Zulus were seen disappearing over a hill to the right of it, looking like an enormous mass of ants or swarm of bees, so we were halted for a few minutes to let the artillery send a few shells into them. We saw every shell burst right in the middle of them, but the mass was so dense that whatever gaps were caused by the shot were instantly filled up and it was impossible to see what damage had been done. Anyone who has handled a swarm of bees would see the simile.

– CHAPTER 3 –
RORKE'S DRIFT

IT WAS QUITE DARK when the Force reached the now devastated camp. On the right, where I was with the 2nd Battalion, 3rd N.N.G., the grass on the undulating ground over which we advanced had been trampled quite flat and smooth by the Zulu army, but no dead were lying about, so without doubt they must have carried off their own casualties. On the left, towards the "neck" where the 24th and others of our men made their stand, the dead lay thick, and it was a ghastly sight. Had it not been for the seriousness of the situation, the manner in which my lot of the N.N.C. had to be driven along would have been amusing. A two-deep line formation was not at all to their liking, all were in a most mortal funk, nothing on earth could make those who were armed with rifles keep their place in the front rank, and all the curses showered on them by their officers could not prevent them from closing in and mixing up in clumps. I had an awful time of it, too, directly it got dusk, doing nothing but ride from one end of the line-to the other, hustling them on to prevent lagging. How Lonsdale and his lot got on I don't know, but no doubt had the same trouble having got into the camp and meeting with no resistance.

The Troops were ordered to bivouac on the ground, and a large hollow square was formed on the "neck" across the main road, a deep valley running down between us and the opposite hill behind which Dabulamanzi with a considerable *impi* lay hidden. The greater portion of the Zulu army which had taken part in the massacre in the camp, we learnt afterwards, had gone straight off to Kambula, sixty miles away, that night, to attack Colonel Evelyn

Wood's column the next morning. To the 2nd Battalion, 3rd N.N.G. was assigned the rifle face of the square which rested at the foot of the slope running down from Isandhlwana hill itself, and the men kept in mass formation in quarter column. The night was pitch dark, and the stench, which was mostly from the smashed-up contents of the Royal Army Medical Corps wagon containing all manner of chemicals, within a few yards of us, was truly awful. As soon as the bivouac had settled down - and by this time the Zulus had begun to light fires and could be seen moving about on the ridge just across the valley, barring our line of retreat to Rorke's Drift - Lord Chelmsford himself took a look round to see how things were going. On coming across to us he had many questions to ask concerning the Contingent, and stayed talking for some

Sir Evelyn Wood.

time, among other things asking me what I thought the Zulus would do, whether they would attack us or not, and I told him that I felt pretty certain that they would as soon as it was daylight.

Later on during the night he paid us another visit, just after a nice escapade by our terrorised Natives. What happened was this. At a quiet moment, when I saw my way to getting away for a few minutes, I hurriedly stole out into the camp to the spot where my tent had rested, to see if I could find any of my belongings lying about, and on returning to the bivouac found that nearly the whole of our Natives had disappeared as by magic. Curiously, no-one had noticed them as they squatted, gently and gradually sliding down the hill into the valley like a huge landslide, notwithstanding the inky darkness of the night and the fact that the moving mass consisted of some 800 men or more. It was an uncommonly serious state of affairs, and might have given rise to a false alarm at any moment, so after sending some of our own officers off to give immediate warning of what had taken place to the troops near us, I bolted down the hill as quickly as I could. Inky dark as it was, I managed by degrees to stumble on clumps of men here and there, and many of the dark figures I ran up against, who were not squatting, I feel certain were Zulus and not our men. Anyway, I was never interfered with.

After a good deal of trouble I rounded up at all events the majority of the men, and literally drove them back to the square. Scarcely had they been got into position again than the General paid us another visit, and I had to tell him what had taken place. He was very angry, and said, "I will give you two men of the 24th Regiment", and sending for them at once placed them himself as sentries, with orders to bayonet the first Native that attempted to move from his position, and directing me in his presence to explain this to the men. After this there was no further trouble.

The visit to my tent proved a blank, everything had gone, and the same with Lonsdale's tent, which was next to it, but between our tents lay the bodies of two artillery men, disembowelled and terribly mutilated.

Within a few yards of where our wagon had been drawn up I found the dead bodies of our two drivers, with their faces blackened, and it struck me at the time that they must have done this themselves in the hope of being able to escape. On passing the hospital wagon from whence all the abominable stench came, I came across the body of Surgeon-Major Shepherd, the P.M.O., who in years gone by had been Assistant-Surgeon in the 99th Regiment. He was lying face downwards, and had been stabbed in the neck, but his body had not been mutilated.

Several times during the night Major Clery, the Adjutant-General, came over and had a talk, and on one of these occasions we were strolling out on the "neck" when we came across a large tarpaulin rolled up, and being a comfortable-looking seat both of us at once sat down but silently rose up again somewhat horrified on feeling that we had sat on something soft and undoubtedly a dead body. Why we neither of us thought of unrolling the tarpaulin to ascertain whose body it was I don't know, except that under the circumstances of the moment, with dead all around one, we had no stomach for curiosity.

During the night one or two officers of the different Corps were permitted to go off for a short time in search of food, but as the Zulus had turned out the contents of the Commissariat wagon, stabbing or smashing up all the tinned articles and apparently carried off all the biscuits, little or nothing was found. One officer, however, Lieutenant Newnham Davis, of the "Buffs", who was with the Mounted Infantry, managed to get a two-pound tin of corned beef, almost whole, and as we tramped in together to Rorke's Drift the following morning demolished the lot, never offering me or anyone else even a mouthful. I don't think another officer, N.C.O. or Private, in the whole column, would have been guilty of such selfish gluttony.

Imperial Mounted Infantry troopers.

Of course we never saw anything more of the four companies of the N.N.C. that had been left in the Camp, with the exception of the Captain, who had escaped on my little grey pony. Every other European had undoubtedly been killed, but a good many of the Natives from all accounts got away, though they never rejoined us again. Throughout the night we could see the intermittent flashes of light from the firing at the Rorke's Drift post, which was only some three or four miles off in a straight line, though twelve miles by road. Everyone felt very anxious for the fate of the little garrison after what had happened in the Camp, and longed for daylight to march to their relief.

At last the day dawned and the troops began to move off. The Contingent formed the rearguard and were the last to quit the ground, in broad daylight, and it was my business to see the last man away. Contrary to all expectations, Dabulamanzi with his *impi* made no attempt whatever to interfere with the Column, though some hundreds of his warriors sat and stood within a few yards of us on the right of the road, simply gazing at us like sightseers at a review. I and… many others… were absolutely dumbfounded at this extraordinary spectacle, and could scarcely believe our eyes. Personally, I felt very suspicious about it all and thought a trap was being laid, especially as a few hundreds yards below on our left, just above the Buffalo River, great masses of Zulus were coming away from Rorke's Drift who could easily have swept up the hills, joined Dabulamanzi's men, and come down like an avalanche from the rear on our straggling Column.

As we were hurrying along at a great pace, I thought that perhaps the masses of Zulus in the valley below us had escaped the notice of the head of the Column, so rode on as fast as I could, to report. But I found that the General was aware of their presence, and that unless they attacked, the Column was to push on with all haste to Rorke's Drift. Luckily, we got in unmolested. As we approached the Drift and reached the hill overlooking the river and the Post, the excitement became intense, all eyes were strained and field-glasses raised, to see if there was any sign of life in the Fort. Then, as we drew nearer, a man was seen on the bared roof of one of the buildings, signalling with a flag, which was hailed with a tremendous cheer from the whole Column as we knew then that the garrison had not been wiped out.

The General and his staff galloped off at once to the Fort and the troops got in by degrees, the selecting of their camping grounds taking some little time. We were the last to get in, and for some time it was quite impossible to keep the men in hand. They were all round the surroundings of the Fort in a second, crowding about the Zulu dead who were lying thick everywhere, partly, no doubt, from curiosity but I dare say some may have been looking out to identify friends or relations as many of the Natal Kaffirs are refugees from Zululand.

Commandant Lonsdale having gone to interview the General and to get something to eat, I also strolled into the Fort and helped myself bountifully to some biscuits, several boxes of which the thoughtful Commissariat Officers, Dunne and Dalton, had hauled out and opened for us hungry souls. What a Godsend it was, as it was over two days and two nights since most of us had had a mouthful of food. Hunger, however, luckily does not affect one like thirst, and one could have gone on much longer as there was plenty of good water.

As I ate biscuits I wandered about the Fort, looking at the wreckage which gave the appearance and feeling of devastation after a hurricane, with the dead bodies thrown in, the only thing that remained whole being a circular miniature fortress constructed of bags of mealies in the centre. Several of our dead lay just where they had fallen, and one of them - a youngster in the Natal Mounted Police - a very fine specimen of humanity, struck me particularly. Having given our natives ample time to exhaust their curiosity, they were got together and marched off to the position allotted to us at the back of the Fort, behind the Itchiane hill to guard the valley up which the Zulus had made their attacks, well hidden until the last moment. Outposts were at once posted and Mounted Patrols sent out, and the remainder of the troops not thus occupied were told off to clear the surroundings of the Fort and renovate the defences. As many of our men as could be supplied with picks and shovels were set to work to dig pits and bury the dead Zulus, and the remainder brought in stones for reconstructing and strengthening the barricades. Altogether, it was a stiff day, and officers and men worked alike.

The General left very shortly for Helpmekaar, en route for Picter-maritzburg, leaving Colonel Glyn in command with Major Clery as Chief Staff Officer, and Colonel Degacher then took over the command of the 24th Regiment. Before leaving, the General issued orders for the disbandment of the Natives of the Contingent, and leave was granted to Commandant Lonsdale to proceed to Cape Town for the purpose of raising a Mounted Corps (but I don't think this was carried out), and he left us. The orders regarding myself were, that I was to remain for duty in charge of the European Officers and N.C.O.'s of the Contingent until they had all been drafted off to other columns, after which I was to rejoin my Regiment with No. 1 Column on the Coast. The matter of collecting arms and equipment from our men was taken in hand at once, and took some little time. They were all, of course, allowed to retain their blankets, much to their joy - and with as much beef as they could stuff themselves with the night before being set free, all were in the highest spirits. I shall never forget the scene at their departure, we started them off soon after sunrise, and the whole mass of some 3,000 bounded gaily off, laughing and joking and performing all sorts of antics, then presently dividing into separate parties, making bee-lines for their homes, very soon presented the appearance of swarms of ants covering the hillsides.

The defence of Rorke's Drift 1879. Oil painting by Alphonse de Neuville in 1880.

A considerable number went via Helpmekaar, and here a most amusing, though at the same time rather an alarming, situation was created. There being no telegraphic communication between Helpmekaar and Rorke's Drift, and the staff at Rorke's Drift having quite forgotten to send a messenger to let the O.C. Helpmekaar know that the Contingent were being disbanded - their outpost took our men to be a Zulu *impi* advancing, and sent in reports to that effect. This of course caused the Helpmekaar garrison to man their defences and prepare for a fight. Several shots, I believe, were fired at our men by the outposts, but luckily no-one was hit. Someone, however, before the outposts retired, discovered in some way that the supposed enemy were men of the Contingent, but the Helpmekaar garrison had had a good fright.

With the disbandment of our men, the officers and N.C.O.'s of the Contingent were brought into the Fort and given the N.E. corner of it to hold, and a very tight fit it was for everyone as the place-was overcrowded with the number of men in occupation. To make matters worse we had a lot of rain, and the interior of the Fort became a simple quagmire from the tramping of so many feet. Fatigue parties were employed for the best part of the day in carrying liquid mud away and emptying the slush outside. In this state of filth we lived and ate and slept for more than two months, no-one being in possession of anything more than a blanket and the clothes that he stood up in. An exception was made, however, with 13 Company, 2nd battalion 24th Regiment, who had made such a gallant defence, and they were housed in the attic of Rorke's house with a tarpaulin thrown over the rafters (from which the thatch had been removed) to shelter them from the wet, a well-deserved honour. However, even they had their troubles in trying to keep dry, as the tarpaulin often bagged in between the rafters with a collection of water which had to be ejected, and I shall not easily forget one particular night when Dr. Reynolds, who got the V.C., and I met in the dark having been literally washed out of our sleeping place, and mooched about, endeavouring to find a more sheltered spot. Suddenly we hit upon the idea of lying down under the eaves of B. Company's roof, so coiled ourselves up in our soaking wet blankets, thanking our stars that at all events there would be no river running under us, when presently swish came about half a ton of water clean on top of us - B. Company were emptying their tarpaulin! It was useless moving, as we could not better ourselves, and wet as we were, thanks to the temperature of the atmosphere and the heat from our bodies, were comfortably warm as long as we lay still.

This terrible state of things, living in such slush, caused a lot of sickness from fever and dysentery which carried off a large number of men and one or two of the officers. Notwithstanding this, and the knowledge that the Fort was overcrowded, Colonel Glyn declined to have any tents pitched outside to relieve matters, being afraid that the Zulus might sweep down on the place again; and so conscientiously did he believe that this would happen that no-one but the officers and N.C.O.'s of the Contingent were allowed outside the Fort. The officers of the Contingent being all mounted, it fell to our lot to perform all the reconnoitring and patrolling work, and at dawn every morning while the garrison stood to their arms we issued out to scour the surrounding country for a mile or two, closely examining the ground everywhere, which was not altogether a pleasant undertaking at that hour of the day. Then, returning to get something to eat and feed the horses, we again saddled up, and dividing into two parties started to patrol and reconnoitre the river, one lot going up towards Helpmekaar and the other down towards the "Fugitives' Drift" - so-called from being the crossing by which all who escaped from Isandhlwana made their way.

The distance that each patrol covered was from eight to ten miles, and on returning, verbal reports were made to Major Clery, the Chief of the Staff. Some 300 or 400 yards behind the Fort, and overlooking it, was Itchiane hill from the summit of which a splendid panorama of the country for a great many miles round could be obtained, and where, after the arrival of the relief column a heliograph station was established. On the morning of the Isandhlwana fight, the Rev. George Smith went up there to see what was going on, as he had heard the guns in the distance, and a day or so after we got in he took me up to explain to me what he had seen. On the "neck" just below Isandhlwana hill he saw the artillery firing, and presently a large body of Natives moving round the hill towards them. Thinking it was our Contingent, he said to himself, "Well done, Lonsdale!", as they were moving with such precision. Then shortly after, he noticed a number of horsemen galloping for their lives, away on his right, making towards the Drift, which made him think that Lord Chelmsford's column were being driven back, and almost at the same time large numbers of Natives appeared away to his left front, coming up from the river very leisurely and massing in the valley. After taking a look at these, and seeing that none of them wore the red head-band of Lonsdale's men, his first impulse was to go down and parley with them, but noticing that their numbers were considerably increasing he hastened down the hill again to inform Chard and Bromhead who, however, had already received warning that a Zulu *impi* was advancing on the Fort. The horsemen he had seen were fugitives from the Camp and had passed the Post before he got down, and be it to their everlasting shame and dishonour, galloped on as hard as they could, refusing to stop a moment to assist the garrison, and merely shouted out that the Zulus were close on them. How far their flight took them, I don't think was ever ascertained.

The part which the Rev. Mr. Smith played in the defence, and the splendid example he set throughout that terrible night, ought to have earned for him the V.C. The same with the Acting Commissariat Officer, Mr. James Dalton, who in the absence of Lieutenant Chard, R.E., (who was down at the river…

superintending Pontoon work at the moment when warning was received of the nearness of the Zulus), devised all the rapid arrangements for the defence as well as working like a Trojan himself with the men at the barricades and did much gallant work during the night. All this was gratefully acknowledged by Lieutenant Chard in his report to the Commander-in-Chief after the fight, but neither Dalton nor Smith received any further distinction than promotion. Mr Thomas Atkins is the best judge of gallant deeds, and when he applauds you may be certain that he is right and does so with good reason, and I noticed that directly Mr Smith or Mr Dalton showed themselves they received an ovation from the men, which was unmistakable.

Engraving of Lieutenant John Rouse Merriott Chard (1847-1897) who commanded the troops at Rorke's Drift, where he won a VC.

Among the six or seven young soldiers of the 24th who garrisoned the hospital and received the V.C. for defending it against such tremendous odds, and removing most of the sick while absolutely surrounded by Zulus, was one named Hook, who was taken on as servant by Major Black, whose shrill voice with its Scotch accent could be heard above the Fort calling for "H-o-o-k!" many times a day. So the men had their little joke, and whenever Hook was called for they themselves shouted for Hook and then yelled out, "I think he's hooked it, sir!", which always caused great merriment.

The following astounding incident of Colonel Harness's servant's escape from the hands of the Zulus was told me by one

Engraving of Lieutenant Gonville Bromhead (1845-1892) who was second in command at Rorke's Drift where he won a VC.

of the garrison; Colonel Harness, C.R.A. of the 3rd Column, had been obliged to leave his servant behind sick at Rorke's Drift when the Column crossed into Zululand, and on the night of the attack on the Fort he happened to be outside the barricades at the moment when the Zulus made their sudden rush on the hospital. As he would to a certainty have been shot down by the fire of our own men had he attempted in the darkness to run in and clamber back again, he quickly bolted under a small hand-cart that had accidentally been left propped up outside against the back of the hospital wall and which (luckily for him, but unfortunately for the garrison), was in such a position as to be completely out of the line of fire. Here he remained throughout the night, wrapped up in his blanket, with the Zulus swarming all round him - many of them actually jumping on to the cart to try and get on to the roof of the hospital, which some of them succeeded in doing and setting fire to it. But none of them, curiously enough, made any attempt to move the cart, in which case he would have been done for. In the morning, however, when the Zulus had decamped and all firing had ceased, to the great astonishment of the garrison he walked in safe and sound, after about as terrifying an experience as any man could have gone through.

By another lucky coincidence, too, the whole garrison had escaped a terrible catastrophe as only a very short distance away at the back of the Fort, between it and the Itchiane hill, a large hay rick had been left standing, there being no time to clear it away before the Zulus commenced their attack, which if they had fired it would have smoked everyone out and rendered the Fort enterable; but luckily, in their eagerness to wipe out the garrison with the assegai, it was left untouched.

After some little time, Colonel Glyn left and the command devolved on Colonel Degacher, Major Black taking over command of the 2nd Battalion, 24th Regiment. A completely new regime was now established; everyone was cleared out of the Fort, tents

'Rorke's House Front View, Buffalo River', 1879.

were pitched, and an encampment formed outside. No more living in mud and slush, and a marked decrease of sickness was the result.

Now no sooner had the whole place been thoroughly cleaned up than a plague of flies set upon us, which was truly awful, and bad as it was for us human beings it was ten thousand times worse for the wretched ponies and mules, for whom we kept smoky fires going all day to try and keep the scourges off them as much as possible, but it was of very little avail. From sheer worry, the poor beasts lost flesh to such an extent that their bones protruded as if they had been starved.

For us, too, it was a terrible state of things, the brutes were everywhere and got into our pots and pans even while the food was being cooked. To get a cup of tea or coffee one had to cover the tea-cup with one's hand, leaving only enough room for the spout of the kettle while someone else poured the tea in, and even then they got in. But the worst part of all this was that in nine cases out of ten food was ejected almost as soon as it was swallowed. Unfortunately, there was not a sufficient supply of disinfectant to cope with matters, so nothing could be done. Naturally, towards evening the flies all went off to sheltered spots for the night, and many millions got inside the tent, only to get a very warm reception. One mode of procedure was to get rid of them thus: after peeping into the tent and seeing a black mass covering the top to about three feet or more, three or four of us would enter quietly, close up the tent and each with a torch made of paper, grass or anything that would give a flame, light these and then quickly, altogether, rush them. In this way we slew many thousands every evening.

- CHAPTER 4 -
RECOVERY OF THE QUEEN'S COLOUR

VERY SOON AFTER THE relief column got to Rorke's Drift, rumours got abroad - how, I don't know - that Lieutenants Melvill and Coghill, of the 1st Battalion, 24th Regiment had been seen escaping from the camp at Isandhlwana with the Colours. One rumour said that the Colours were on their staffs, and another that they had wrapped the Colours under their uniforms, round their bodies. This gave special interest to our patrol work in the direction of Fugitives' Drift, and I made it my business to accompany any patrol every day and keep an eye on the state of the river, which kept in flood for a long time at that time of the year from heavy thunderstorms up-country.

Those of us who were not on patrol duty assisted in renovating and adding to the defences of the Fort and putting up enclosures for the animals, and as soon as an opportunity offered, a Prize Committee of Officers and N.C.O.'s of the Contingent was ordered to assemble to assess the value of the captured cattle, sheep and goats. These were all bought by a Mr Button, a butcher and trader from Maritzburg, for £3,000, and we heard a short time afterwards that before he had returned to Maritzburg he had sold the cattle alone for £40,000. A nice little fortune. What became of the £3,000 none of us ever heard, anyhow none of us ever received any Prize money.

I forget now what brought Captain Jones, R.E. to Rorke's Drift, but while he was with us he managed to obtain through the General's interpreter a very interesting account of how it was that the Zulus did not attack us at Isipezi, and also how it was that no attempt was made to interfere with Lord Chelmsford's march to the relief of Rorke's Drift - from a Zulu prisoner. The man said that the Zulu *impi* which confronted us at Isipezi had been ordered by Cetewayo to wipe out all the "redcoats" of Lord Chelmsford's column, and were on their way to attack the camp at Isandhlwana when we came across them. They saw that we were not "redcoats", but only Police Volunteers and Natives, so they left us alone, intending to come back and wipe us out after they had finished with the Camp. So this is how we escaped disaster at Isipezi.

Now for the reason why Lord Chelmsford, with the remnants of his Column, was not interfered with on the march in to the relief of Rorke's Drift. After the massacre at the Camp, messengers had been at once sent back to Cetewayo to say that the whole camp had been wiped out, and not a "redcoat" left alive, but when late in the afternoon we, with the seven companies of the 24th and some artillery, were seen advancing on the camp the Zulus became thoroughly alarmed and said, "Didn't we kill every 'redcoat' in the Camp, and haven't we sent word to Cetewayo to say so, then how is it that these 'redcoats' we see are still alive? They must have come to life again!"

So, during the night Dabulamanzi held a council of war, at which all the younger men were for attacking us in the morning but the older warriors agreed that it would be quite useless to fight men who could rise again from the dead, so it was decided that we were not to be interfered with. Hence the extraordinary spectacle that we had witnessed, of a Zulu *impi* actually at war with us standing by the roadside, quietly watching us on the march without raising a finger. Lord Chelmsford's night march to our assistance at Isipezi had completely baffled them; having under cover of darkness left the camp and made his way along the plains, nothing had been seen of his movements. They themselves,

'Sketch of Lord Chelmsford made by an officer shortly before the battle of Ulundi.'
Frederick Thesiger, 2nd Baron Chelmsford (1827 – 1905)

in their eagerness to completely surprise the camp, had made a tremendous detour throughout the night, hidden behind a far range of hills without throwing out any feeler towards the lower ground. Consequently, they knew nothing of any troops having left the Camp, and imagined that on their attack on the camp they had killed every "redcoat" belonging to the Column.

Our daily occupation of patrolling the river kept us in excellent health and spirits, and was most interesting. The landscape all round was simply magnificent, and the scent from the different flowering shrubs and grasses, especially the tambooti grass, in the warm atmosphere was too delicious for anything. I used to long for my gun when a buck jumped up, but alas, my two beautiful weapons - a twelve and an eleven bore from George Gibbs, of Bristol - together with every other of my belongings, had been lost in the Camp.

Isandhlwana hill and the "neck" on which we had slept on the night of the disaster was always in sight, together with the hospital wagon which showed up clearly against the skyline and which, for some reason or another, the Zulus had left alone and had never made any attempt to remove. A sharp eye was kept on all the ground in that direction, and for the first week or so small parties of Zulus could be seen clearly through our glasses, wandering about, searching the place all over, no doubt, for either full or empty cartridges. Several were dressed in white shirts, some of which were undoubtedly my property, as I had a dozen new ones in my portmanteau.

Notwithstanding the fact that some of the enemy were still hanging about in the vicinity, the whole of the men of the garrison were eager to march back to Isandhlwana and bury the dead, but the authorities considered that too great a risk would be run, so, much to the regret of all, the dead were left where they lay.

Traps were often set for our Patrols by the Zulus, in the hope of catching us tripping. Cattle were driven up into enticing places in the hope that we might try and capture them, seeing that there was no-one with them. This was their favourite ruse, but occasionally they lodged their women and children, partially concealed in the bush, from whence a rush could have been made had we been such idiots as to go anywhere near them. But on only one occasion during the whole of our patrolling did we have a scare, which luckily ended without any unpleasant incident. We happened to drop on a mealie garden which we had not come across before, with the stalks still standing, and thinking that we might with luck find

Prince Dabulamanzi KaMpande, Cetywayo's half-brother.

a cob or two and perhaps a stray vegetable of some sort, we got off our ponies, which we left outside to graze as they were all reliable shooting ponies, and went into the field, which was situated on the side of a little hollow just above a deep krantz overlooking the river. I suppose we must have been searching about for a quarter of an hour, when suddenly within about thirty yards or so of me I saw a Native crop up out of the krantz and stand with his shield raised above his head, scanning the ground all round. I thought to myself, "Now we are in a nice mess!", so I lay flat on my stomach. Young Wainwright, one of my officers, was not far from me, and I beckoned to him to get down and come up to me, pointing at the same time towards the Native. As soon as he had crawled up we had a short consultation, and in the meanwhile some four or five more Natives had come up and it looked very much as if we had been spotted and were being surrounded.

Having quickly arranged our plans, we rose up and quietly walked out of the field towards our ponies as if we had seen nothing, and called to the remainder of our party that we were going off, and to come in at once. Then catching our ponies, we got on and rode very quietly up the hill, waiting for the others to mount. When we had put a good hundred yards between the Natives and ourselves I ordered a halt, and sent two of our party to scout a little distance back, along the krantz, to see if an attempt was being made to cut off our retreat, everything looking so suspicious and the group at the edge of the krantz having made no attempt to move. Scarcely had we halted than several other Natives joined the group, one of them carrying a large green flag. This was most puzzling, as Zulus carry no standards, but we thought it was only a further blind to trap us, and I'm ashamed to say that at this juncture one of the officers of my patrol turned tail and went back to Rorke's Drift as hard as his pony could carry him.

Seeing the peculiar behaviour of the Natives, I decided to call on them to surrender and told them to come up to us with their flag, but for some time they made no answer or any attempt to move. At last I called down to them that if they didn't come up and surrender at once we should fire on them, whereupon the man carrying the flag, escorted by two or three of the others of the group, advanced towards us and halted when within a few yards of us. We now learnt that they belonged to Major Bengough's Contingent and had been sent on ahead to scout towards Rorke's Drift, as the Contingent were marching up in that direction. So, after telling them that no-one had received any intimation of Major Bengough's coming, and that they had had a precious narrow squeak from being shot, we went our several ways. It was an adventure, and but for the disgraceful act of one solitary individual, we had got out of the mess all right.

Occasionally I rode out by myself to take a look round, and one afternoon about a mile from the Fort came across a portmanteau torn in half and empty, but lying by the side of it was a Bible, and a few feet further on a silver watch, which I restored to their rightful owner, the Rev. Mr Smith, when I got back, and very pleased he was to have them in his possession again. The portmanteau itself was far too damaged to be of any further use, so was left where it was.

The same day, I think it was, I came across the body of a very fine specimen of a Zulu in the skeleton stage, which I took Surgeon Reynolds out to have a look at. He too was impressed with the stature and splendid proportions, and brought away one or two bones of Scientific interest, and the soles of the feet which had become detached and were just like solid pieces of horn. I also took one of the collar bones and the lesser bones of one of the arms, which I intended some day to give to the Durban Museum.

In the year of grace 1879, subaltern officers were of very small account, and in my position of Staff Officer to a Native Contingent, (with the honorary rank of Captain while so employed), and consequently an outsider, one did not expect very much from anyone, but the kindness and hospitality extended to me by the 24th Regiment very soon made me feel almost as one of them, and many lasting friendships was the result. I remember Lieutenants Smylie, Phipps and Geoghegan joining us at Rorke's Drift, the latter becoming a Captain within a month or two, through death vacancies. Major Black became an especially intimate friend of mine, and I could always go to him for advice and to talk over matters. Besides being a splendid soldier he was a most amusing companion, and his fondness for bringing in lines of poetry to suit the occasion was a treat to listen to, with his Gaelic accent.

The necessity of keeping our clothes (which were none other than what we stood up in), as clean as we could, without such luxury as soap, we often went down to the river together, washed our things and swam about… till they were dry - which was not a long process on warm rocks with a nice hot sun in addition. But the swimming part came to an end rather abruptly when one day an alligator showed himself some yards above us, with his head just out of the water, and made us skedaddle at our best swimming pace. Though, as John Dunn taught me, when bathing with him at the Lower Tugela where the river was literally swarming with them, they will never come near you as long as you keep up a tremendous amount of splashing.

In front of the Fort and some 600 or 700 yards down the slope of the hill, a scaffold had been put up by the Commissariat Department on which the carcasses of the cattle were hung up previous to issue, and one morning Major Black and I were sitting outside, warming ourselves in the sun and chatting, when we saw a most extraordinary-looking object suspended on the scaffold, and wondered what on earth it could be. Presently, a Private of the 24th came up from that direction, and Black asked him what the thing was, and he said that it was a Kaffir spy that had been hanged. "Good Heavens!", said Black, "By whose orders was he hung?" "Captain Harford, sir", was the reply, so we went down at once to look into the matter. The poor wretch, who was an old, wizened-up, grey-headed Native, had apparently been dead for some hours, and must have been hung some time during the night, but by whom it was never discovered. Every possible enquiry was made, but not a soul knew anything about it and nothing was known of the Native or where he could have come from.

As time went on the river got lower, and at last became shallow enough to enable our patrols almost to count with the naked eye articles of debris of every description with which the now bare shingle was strewn at the Fugitives' Crossing - saddles, bridles, stirrups, helmets, clothing, boots and numbers of other things could be seen, but no sign of the 24th Regiment's lost Colours. It was now clear that measures should be taken in hand at once to search for them, and I reported this to Major Clery. Colonel Glyn, however, for some reason of his own, declined to allow a search party to be organised by the 24th, and I, on the other hand, felt very unwilling to carry out a mission which - subaltern only, as I was - I considered would be anything but creditable to the Regiment, they being actually on the spot. Had I been ambitious for self-advertisement, I should have said no more and simply undertaken the job with my own officers and N.C.O.'s, all of whom were as keen as possible for the outing. So I talked matters over with Major Black, and asked him to use his influence with Colonel Glyn, and see what could be done.

I had returned from patrolling on this particular day early, in order that no time should be lost in arranging about a search party going out the next morning. Major Black's interview, happily, ended in Colonel Glyn giving him permission to go out in command of our Contingent, and his face beamed with delight when he came out to tell me the news. As we had all had our frugal meal, and the afternoon was before us, he at once said, "Come along, we'll saddle up and you show me the ground", so he and I went off on a most enjoyable and interesting ride. Having been confined to the vicinity of the Fort for so long, our spirits rose high as we cantered across country, watching the surroundings of Isandhhwana and speculating on the morrow's adventure.

On coming to the spot which overlooked the crossing, we first of all had a good look with our glasses at the mass of debris lying about, and then walked about to examine the ground with a view to finding a good position for a covering-party to be placed while the actual search-party were down in the river bed. Having arranged this, and as there was still sufficient of the afternoon left, Major Black suggested that we should go a little further down, following as well as we could over the stony and precipitous ground, the Kaffir path by which, it was said, the fugitives had made their way. Suddenly, just off the track to the right of us, we saw two bodies, and on going to have a look at them, found that they were those of Lieutenants Melvill and Coghill! Both were clearly recognisable. Melvill was in red, and Coghill in blue, uniform. Both were lying on their backs about a yard from each other, Melvill at right angles to the path and Coghill parallel to it, a little above Melvill and with his head up-hill. Both had been assegaied, but otherwise their bodies had been left untouched.

Major Black at once said, "Now we shall see whether they have the Colours on them", and proceeded to unbutton Melvill's serge, while I opened Coghill's patrol jacket, but there were no Colours. Presently Major Black said, "I wonder if Melvill's watch is on him! He always carried it in the small waist-pocket of his breeches!", and on looking, there was his gold watch, which was subsequently sent to his widow. Nothing was found on Coghill, but his bad knee was still bandaged up. Undoubtedly, Melvill must have stuck to him and helped him along, otherwise he never could have got so far over such terrible ground.

Our search over, we set to work at once to cover the bodies with large stones and bits of rock, for protection till proper interment could take place, after which we rode home, as it was getting dusk. It was a memorable afternoon, and had made it certain that neither Melvill or Coghill had the Colours about their persons. Our news, on getting back, naturally caused a good deal of interest and excitement, and speculation as to the result of tomorrow's expedition.

Soon after sunrise the following morning our little cavalcade of officers and N.C.O.'s of the Contingent, headed by Major Black in command, and myself, moved quietly away. Orders had been given to the signallers stationed on the top of Itchiane hill, who could see almost the whole of our route with their telescope, to keep an eye in our direction and signal down to the Fort anything of importance concerning our movements. Captain Raw was the senior of the officers of the Contingent, and when we arrived on the ground chosen by Major Black for the covering-party to establish themselves on, a substantial sangar of rocks and stones was soon built up and he was given charge of the party.

Major Black now decided Captain Harber and Lieutenant Wainwright should accompany me to the river bed and carry out the search operations. After a tremendous climb down, and on getting to the bottom of the krantz, we found ourselves at the corner of a delta formed by the river, which was now dry shingle and covered with every imaginary article of equipment discarded by the fugitives as they crossed the swirling stream, as well as other species of debris. Losing no time, I told off Harber to walk downstream close to the river edge, and Wainwright to follow the curve of the delta, while I moved through the centre. We were thus only a few yards apart, and it was unlikely that anything would escape detection.

Scarcely had we taken a few steps than I stumbled on the Colour case mixed up with a heap of other things, and picking it up I said to Harber, who was closest to me, "Look here, here's the case! The Colours can't be far off!" We all three then had a look at it, put it on a conspicuous boulder, and went on. Then, as

Harber was returning to his position, I noticed a straight piece of stick projecting out of the water in the middle of the river, almost in a line with us, and said to him, "Do you see that straight bit of stick sticking up in the water opposite to you? It looks to me uncommonly like a Colour pole." He waded straight in, up to his middle, and got hold of it. On lifting it out he brought up the Colour still adhering to it, and on getting out of the water handed the standard to me, and as he did so the gold-embroidered centre scroll dropped out, the silk having more or less rotted from the long immersion in the water. Our cheers very soon brought Major Black tearing down the krantz as fast as precipitous rocks, boulders and thorn bush would allow him, and in the meanwhile we continued our search in the hope of dropping across the other Colour, as two had been lost, but without any further luck. Major Black having got down to us, I handed him the Colour amid ringing cheers in which he joined, and after having congratulated

'Recovery of Colour of 24th Regiment' by Harford.
(London Illustrated News)

and thanked us, and shaken us well by the hand, we proceeded to climb back to the covering party, he carrying the Colour.

It was a real business getting up, but he gave us such an entertaining time of it in our scramble that little heed was taken of the difficulties of the situation. On getting up to them, Captain Raw and his party drew up, and after saluting the Colour gave three times three for Her Majesty, the Queen, and ourselves. The ponies were now got together and saddled up, and we returned back to the Fort in the following formation: Major Black leading, carrying the cased Colour erect, the butt of the Standard resting on the right stirrup, so that the signallers on Itchiane hill could make no mistake. Harbcr and Wainwright and I followed at some twenty yards' interval, and the rest of the party about the same distance in rear of us.

We knew that the sight of the Colour would cause some excitement at the Fort, but I don't think any of us expected the little surprise reception that awaited us there. A Guard of Honour was stationed outside at the entrance, and the whole garrison turned out to give us an ovation. It certainly was a triumphal return, but I suppose with the exception of Major Black none of us thought of the significance of the occasion. Speaking for myself personally, I felt that we had had a most enjoyable and exciting day, and the luck in recovering the Colour gave one the same feelings of pleasure as one experiences in capturing a new or rare butterfly or having got up to an almost inaccessible nest and brought the egg safely down.

Captain Symons made a sketch of the scene on our arrival, which appeared in one of the illustrated papers. The sketches that I made of the recovering of the Colour, and the burial of the bodies of Melvill and Coghill, and Otto de Witt's house at Rorke's Drift, all of which were considerably altered by the engraver, appeared in *The Illustrated London News* in the issue dated 12th April, 1879. I really sent these sketches to dear old Jameson, never thinking of publication, but he sent them on to the Publishers.

After a day or two, an escort consisting of Major Black and myself, with a Sergeant of the 24th to carry it, were detailed in orders to convey the Colour to Helpmekaar for the purpose of restoring it to the Battalion, which was quartered there, and for me this ride was to be an ever-memorable event. From the Fort to Helpmekaar was about eleven miles, and after having covered some two or three of them Major Black stopped for a moment and, after making me a delightful little speech referring to my share in the undertaking, took the Colour from the Sergeant and handed it to me to carry for the rest of the journey, saying, "It is nothing but your right." It was the proudest moment of my life, and I shall ever consider it so. I very much doubt whether such another case has ever occurred that an officer on duty and belonging to another Regiment has been given the honour of carrying its Queen's Colour. This same Colour when the 24th Regiment returned to England, was crowned by Her Majesty, Queen Victoria, with a

'Burial of Lieuts. Melvill and Coghill' by Harford.
(London Illustrated News)

wreath of silver laurels and sanctioned by her to be carried on Parade as a Third Colour.

At Helpmekaar the Regiment was drawn up in line to receive us on the heights, and as we rode on to the ground Major Black took the Colour and advanced with it towards the centre. The officer detailed to receive it then came forward, and having received it faced the Line, when the Regiment "presented arms". The officers and Colour having joined the ranks, Major Black proceeded to address the Regiment in a remarkably eloquent speech which must have stirred the feelings of every officer and man who had the privilege of listening to it. This concluded the ceremony, and thus was concluded a truly memorable and historical event.

- CHAPTER 5 -

RETURN TO THE 99TH REGIMENT

IN COURSE OF TIME, when reliefs were about to take place, I was ordered to move to Helpmekaar with what remained of the Contingent, a welcome change to higher ground. We were camped a short distance away from the Laager there, on a treeless plateau; below us, looking down on the Rorke's Drift road and on our first old camping-ground, was a precipitous krantz of huge rocks and thornbush, but all else was miles and miles of green, rolling, grassy hills. I now felt the loss of my guns and material for collecting, which went in the camp at Isandhlwana, as the rocks were full of rock-rabbits and I saw several Steenbuck and covies of partridge. A herd of some seven or eight Hartebeest, strictly preserved as they are becoming extinct, roamed about undisturbed and occasionally came within sight of the camp. A fine of £100 was the penalty for even firing at one.

A few days after my arrival, Major Upcher, 24th Regiment, commanding the garrison, sent for me and told me that the 4th King's Own Regiment were coming in very soon and that the Commissariat were without any cattle, the contractor having failed to bring any up, which placed him in an awkward fix. He asked me to go off at once with one or two of the Contingent who could speak Dutch, and endeavour to obtain 300 head of cattle from the outlying farms in the district. It was a Sunday, and with a couple of officers I started off about midday and reached the nearest farm about sundown. Being the Sabbath, the doors were closed against us and all supplies refused, so we had to make the best of it, and after looking to the needs of our ponies coiled ourselves up in our blankets on the verandah of the house and listened to the family at their prayers and singing hymns to the accompaniment of a harmonium.

In the morning, however, they gave us some excellent coffee, milk and bread and butter, these latter items being an immense treat, many months having elapsed since we had tasted such luxuries. No cattle, however, were obtained at this farm, as the owner declared that they had only very recently been inoculated. Altogether, we were away about a fortnight, riding through beautiful scenery and visiting a great many farms before we got the number of cattle we required. Our furthest point came within a few miles of Ladysmith, and nearly everywhere the veld hospitality was extended to us. I had never before had an opportunity of seeing anything of Boer family life, so thoroughly enjoyed our mission.

Before leaving Helpmekaar, Major Upcher never told me (and I and my two officers entirely forgot to ask him), how much he was in a position to pay per head for the cattle, but as we all three knew what a fortune the contractor had made out of our captured beasts and that there was no reason except gain for his having left the troops in the lurch, we decided among ourselves to teach him a lesson and make him pay for it. So, whatever the price was that the different farms asked, we agreed, and some went as far as £20 per head. Each farmer was told the date on which his cattle must be at Helpmekaar, and having procured our 300 head we returned and reported our doings to Major Upcher, who was very pleased and quite satisfied with our arrangement.

But now came an awful shock and catastrophe. The very morning on which the Dutchmen were bringing in their cattle, who should appear on the scene, suddenly and unexpectedly, but Major Brownrigg, the Senior Commissariat officer, who had ridden in from his Headquarters at Greytown to look into the matter of the meat supply. He was an uncommonly peppery gentleman and, bursting with rage at the steps that had been taken by us, blackguarded the Dutchmen all round for the price they had asked for the cattle and declined to pay one penny more than ,£8 a head. Not caring to be mixed up in the row, I went off to my tent and from under the curtain of it watched the proceedings. The Boers, of course, were very angry, and I saw one of them take off his large Dopper hat and fling it down at Brownrigg's feet, and heard him shouting out and calling him every name under the sun. At last, after a tremendous row, they drove all their cattle away, cursing the "damn Englishman" as they went off. I should have been precious sorry to have gone anywhere out in their direction again, unless I wanted a bullet put through me.

It was a great pity that Major Upcher did not stand firm and take the responsibility on himself of keeping the cattle and making the Contractor pay the bill. All the more so, as it turned out only a few weeks later, when a very junior but smart young Commanding Officer, just out from England, was sent for duty to Greytown and, finding that Major Brownrigg was not only feeding the civil community at the expense of the troops and Government, but allowing their horses to be shod free of charge and generally standing in with the contractors, reported the matter to Headquarters. Whereupon, by some extraordinary coincidence, a fire broke out in Major Brownrigg's office, destroying all his account books in addition to stores, so that no trace was left of his illicit dealings. The end of it was that he was dismissed from the Service.

Transport-riders, one of whom told me that he reckoned to clear £300 on his trip, periodically appeared both at Rorke's Drift and Helpmekaar when the lines of communication were free from any chance of attack, and proved to be both a blessing and a curse as they not only brought every sort of article much needed by us all in the shape of clothing and boots and little accessories, but by far the greater portion of their stores consisted of drink. The regular troops of course were kept in hand and could only make their purchases under supervision, but with the Contingent it was a different matter, and directly these wagons arrived no work could be got out of them and it became impossible to keep any state of discipline; all had plenty of money, and they spent it freely. The prices asked for everything were enormous, boots were from £2 to £5 a pair, beer 2/6d a bottle, brandy £1, whiskey and "Cape Smoke" (called "square-rigger" from the shape of the bottle), 15/- and 10/-. Champagne £3, and so on. Nevertheless, wagons were soon emptied.

On one particular occasion an N.C.O. of the Contingent, an oldish man who had been a digger at the Witwatersrand gave us an anxious time and a lot of trouble which ended in rather an amusing episode. He had purchased a whole case of brandy - twelve bottles - and disappeared with it somewhere in the bush, unbeknown to anyone. For a whole week search-parties including myself were out searching every nook and corner to discover his whereabouts, but not a trace could be found of him until one afternoon Lieutenant Wainwright walked over to a small hut about half a mile from the camp, which was right out in the open and which several of us including myself had visited before and found perfectly empty with the exception of an iron bedstead with a mattress on it. On going inside, seeing nothing more than that, he had called out, "Corporal, you come out of this, we know you're hiding somewhere about here!" Suddenly the mattress began to move, and out popped a head from the inside of it, which said, "Ah, hah! It's you, my bold pippin, is it? All right, I'll come out." Wainwright brought him back none the worse for his debauch and a week in the jungle without food.

While at Helpmekaar I got a Helio message from Colonel Welman, asking me if I would take over the Adjutancy of the Regiment again as poor Davison, who had taken over the work from me, had died at Etchowi, and saying that the 99th Regiment were now at the Lower Tugela with No. 1 Column. Of course I accepted at once, and in a very few days received orders to hand over what details of the Contingent remained with me to the Senior officer and rejoin my Regiment without delay. Being in want of a charger, and knowing how difficult it would be to get one down country, I bought a very nice animal, and a splendid shooting horse into the bargain, from one of the Contingent. His colour was a little against him, being a flea-bitten red skimmel, but for real worth he couldn't be beaten. With a mate he would follow like a dog, and required no leading.

My way to the Lower Tugela was via Greytown, Maritzburg and Durban, and my faithful Kaffir. Jim, preferred to make a short cut across country and meet me at Verulam. The day of my departure was another memorable occasion in my existence, for just before starting I was presented by the assembled officers and N.C.O.'s of the Contingent with an illuminated Address, which I shall always consider the most precious of all my belongings. After the ceremony I was escorted by all who had mounts for eighteen miles to Sand Spruit store where, of course, 1 stood them all a good breakfast. From here I was given a very pleasant send-off, and got into Greytown in the evening where, after looking to my horses' needs and having something to eat myself at the hotel, I called and had a chat with my old friend, Willie Wainwright, the Magistrate.

The next evening found me in Maritzburg, and here I had to stay three or four days as I had to give in my pony and Government carbine at the Remount depot, get some money as well as other commissions, which all took time, and during spare moments looked up old friends.

After returning my pony and carbine to Captain Russell, 12th Lancers, the O.C. Remount Depot (who told me that I was the first individual who had returned anything at all), my first visit was to the Command Pay Office, where I called on Mr. White, the Chief Paymaster, and asked him if he could let me have some money as I hadn't a penny to get on with; but as he required a Pay Certificate signed by Commandant Lonsdale, who was some 1 000 miles away in the Old Colony, in order to draw my staff pay amounting to some £90, I could not get that. Then I asked about my ordinary Regimental pay. Couldn't he give me something on that account? But there again, our Regimental Paymaster held my last Pay Certificate, so he could give me no Regimental pay and expressed his regret at not being able to give me any assistance. Then, just as I was leaving the office, evidently seeing the plight I was in, he called me back and said, "Have you any money with your Regimental Agents?" "Yes", I said, "£33". "Well", he replied, "If you will write out a cheque on them, I will cash it for you." So there and then I wrote out a cheque for that amount on Messrs Price and Boustead, who only about two or three months after went smash, so but for this Providential coincidence I should never have seen a penny of my £38 again.

On one of the evenings, somebody, I forget now who, gave a dance to which I was invited, and went. Where I raised a dress suit to go in I also forget, but when I walked into the ballroom, which was full of old friends and familiar faces, not a single soul made any attempt to recognise me - as I still wore my beard! I felt rather shy of introducing myself, so only stayed for five or ten minutes and strolled off, but before getting very far I met Arthur Shepstone and his wife on their way to it, and was hauled back again, this time to dance all night and have a very pleasant time of it.

Being an honorary member of the Maritzburg Club, I went there a few hours after my arrival and was told that a Kaffir had been there daily for weeks past, enquiring for me, not saying what he wanted except that he wished to see me. I left word as to when I should be at the Club again, and when I did, found my friend squatting patiently waiting on the doorstep for my arrival. Getting up and greeting me with the usual salutation of lnkosi, and evidently very pleased at having unearthed me at last, judge my surprise when from an old bundle he produced the left boot of my favourite pair of Dean's field boots, in which was stowed away two pocket handkerchiefs with my name on them - relics from the camp at Isandhlwana which he had picked up at Ulundi, on the battlefield not far from Cetewayo's kraal.

He had belonged to our Contingent, and on the disbandment of the Natives he had made his way to No. 1 Column on the Coast, whence he had apparently attached himself to the 2nd Natal Native Contingent (in which, no doubt, he had pals), and came in for the fight there. Isandhlwana was fought on the 22nd January, and Ulundi on the 4th July, so the Zulus had ample time to carry off the Isandhlwana loot to Ulundi, and no doubt in the confusion of the distribution my pair of boots had got separated and this single boot thrown away. It is quite safe to say that no-one else in the whole of the Forces had boots of similar cut, and my friend, like all other Kaffirs being an observant individual, knew directly he saw it who it had belonged to, and at once brought it away in the hope of being able to find me again and hand it back. This only shows what a good fellow the kraal Kaffir is, and he in particular was.

Ulundi is about eighty miles as the crow flies from Isandhlwana and about two hundred via the Coast road to Maritzburg, so the Zulu army had the honour of carrying my boot (or boots) for over 150 miles, and this good chap had tramped with it another 200 miles on an off-chance. To him, of course, it was of no value whatever, but to me that boot is greatly treasured, both for the remarkable circumstances under which I got it back and as a reminiscence of my days with the 3rd N.N.C. It is now stored with other belongings at Messrs Curtiss & Sons, at Portsmouth. The pocket handkerchiefs, I'm sorry to say, I had to make use of, so they are no more. My good friend, it is needless to say, was amply rewarded for what he had done.

Natal Native Contingent company.

One of the first persons I met after getting into Maritzburg was Captain Stubbs, 32nd Regiment, who was President of the Board on claims for losses at Isandhlwana. He asked me why I had sent in no claims for anything, but evidently it had been mislaid as I had personally forwarded all claims from the Contingent, to which mine was attached. So I made him out another, and hereby hangs a curious tale showing the inexplicable ways of the War Office. As far as my claim was concerned, it was just two years before I heard anything more about it, and then, when the Regiment was in Bermuda, I received an official letter from the War Office, requesting me to give my reasons for claiming £25 on account of articles lost at Isandhlwana. This struck me as a most extraordinary request, and I showed the letter to the Colonel, to whom I explained that although I had only claimed compensation for an ordinary Field Kit as laid down in Sir Garnet Wolseley's *Soldiers' Pocket Book*, I had really lost over £150 worth of things, including my two guns which were worth £50 alone... (As Staff Officer to the Contingent, having been furnished with a wagon to myself, I had taken many more things with me than I was entitled to by regulations.) He said, "Have you any receipts left of your purchases for the campaign ? If so, I should send them all in and simply say that you had only put in for the cost of a regulation Field Kit, but had lost considerably more, as would be seen by the receipts you enclosed for perusal."

The total now, including the two guns, was close on £200, and another six months went by before anything more was heard of the matter, until one morning I received a cheque for £88.10.6d. How the sum had been arrived at it was impossible to say, but anyhow it was a most welcome surprise and came just at the right moment as the high cost of living in Bermuda was ruining us all, our Mess bills running to about £20 a month for absolutely nothing at all.

Such a thing as a scare was unknown to us at Rorke's Drift, though parties of Zulus continued to prowl about in the vicinity long after Isandhlwana, but on my ride down to the Coast I found everywhere - Greytown, Maritzburg and Durban - still suffering from nerves and most of the streets with their barricades still standing. There was one laager between Helpmekaar and Greytown, (known afterwards as "Fort Funk"), where nearly a month after Isandhlwana a night scare took place, when several thousands of rounds of ammunition were expended on what proved in the morning to be nothing but a derelict ox which a fool of a sentry had mistaken for a party of Zulus.

As I passed through the Umvoti County, Captain Townshend's old coffee plantation at Avoca and the adjoining sugar and other estates recalled many happy memories, and the familiar calls of the birds and other denizens of the bush made me long to go round and have a look at some of my old haunts again. The faithful Jim was awaiting my arrival at Verulam, and the whole of the road from here to the Tugela abounded with reminiscences of the glorious time I spent with Dr Ray in 1864 at the Lower Post, now known as Fort Williamson, riding and shooting all over the country and leading a real Colonial life. The same delicious scent from the veld perfumed the air as in those days, and imbued one with indescribable feelings of life and sport. The country was very little changed from what I had remembered of it, except for alterations caused by floods and storms especially along the river courses, and I felt that I would give a good deal to be able to live my early life at the Lower Post and Avoca over again, with its adventures and splendid training for the rough-and-tumble of the world's existence, which has ever since stood me in such good stead. I can never sufficiently thank or show my gratitude to my dear old friends, Dr Ray and Captain Townshend, for having given me really the opportunity of my life in learning to ride and shoot and the art of roughing it and being able to do everything for oneself.

I found my Regiment, together with the 88th, Royal Irish Regiment, encamped close to the Tugela River on the Zululand

Zulu village.

side, and was told by everyone how stout and fit I looked. I think they expected to see a scarecrow arrive, knowing what a rough time the 3rd Column had had of it, but a hard life suits me down to the ground, though not so with most people. The CD. appearance of the majority of my brother officers, who had been living in luxury, getting everything they required, showed very clearly that living in camp, with little or nothing to do and every want supplied, did not make for health, and I could not return the compliment.

Jim became a great favourite with everyone, officers and men, and I was horrified one morning when he turned up dressed in a blue patrol jacket, red silk sash and glengarry cap presented to him by the Colonel, thinking himself no end of a swell. He was very proud of his appearance, which I was not, as Jim in his "moocha" and Jim in his "Kitchen Kaffir" get-up were not the same sort of individual. Nevertheless, I am glad to think he was not spoilt.

Within forty-eight hours of my resuming my duties as Adjutant there was a midnight scare created by a Colour Sergeant, whose voice as I lay in my tent was quite familiar to me though I hadn't heard it for more than a year. I heard him rush out of his tent, saying, "Here they come! Here they come, right down the hill!", and in a very few moments the whole Regiment were in the trenches. The 88th Regiment, who were close on our right, took up the scare and almost at once commenced blazing away at what was found later on to be a clump of palms whose nodding tops had been mistaken against the skyline, in the darkness, for moving Zulus. Our men, luckily, saw nothing to fire at. I was determined that, as far as I was concerned, this should be the last. Everyone's rest disturbed, and standing to arms all night in the trenches, with the certain knowledge that there could be no enemy within 200 or 300 miles was absolutely ridiculous, so I got the whole of the N.C.O.'s together at the first available moment and lectured them pretty strongly on the matter. I gave strict orders that not a soul in the camp was to be disturbed until I had been made acquainted with the details, and that all reports from sentries or outposts were to be brought to me quietly.

This interview had its effect only a very few nights after, when a young officer in command of an outpost near the river sent up an urgent message reporting that hundreds of Zulus were crossing the Tugela a little distance above his post, so I went down to have a look for myself and see what was happening. On reaching the spot, I came upon the youngster in a great state of excitement. "There they are, Sir. There they are! You can see them crossing. They've got lanterns." The phantom Zulus were nothing but myriads of fireflies, and a sight well worth having been turned out of bed to see, but at the same time I had to give my young friend a good lecture on the trouble that he might have caused. With only a little over a year's service, and never having been out of England before in his life, such a thing as flies being able to emit light was a novelty that never entered his head, and it was curious that none of the N.C.O.'s or men of the picquet could not have put him straight.

It would be far better if Latin and Greek were eliminated from the examination papers for youngsters destined for the Service, and a year's residence in India or one of the Colonies insisted on instead, on which questions of some practical use could be set. This would not only be an advantage to the individual, but be a very great gain to the Service and go a long way to prevent regrettable incidents. Money wasted by parents in sending their sons, as a preliminary, to serve in the Militia and subsequently for cramming, could be spent to better purpose (and the cost of such a measure would be far less).

The nervousness of the Headquarters staff, who apparently also entertained the idea that sundry Zulu *impi's* were lurking about only waiting an opportunity to attack our camp, was very clearly shown one day soon after I had rejoined the Regiment. Lieutenant Neville and I went out for a shoot, to try and get a Rietbuck, and passed over some ground that I knew very well and had shot over with John Dunn when staying with Dr Ray. On our return I found a letter awaiting me from the Adjutant-General, expressing the G.O.C.'s surprise that a good soldier like Lieutenant Harford should have gone out shooting in the neighbourhood of the camp, etc. etc., and that such must not occur again. Anything more idiotic could scarcely be conceived. For reconnoitring work no better means could have been devised than to give encouragement to every sportsman in the camp to scour the country for game, but now we were condemned to stew in our tents.

CHAPTER 6

THE CAPTURE OF CETEWAYO

FROM THE TUGELA THE 99th moved to Fort Chelmsford, a little further up the coast, and before we had been there many days I was offered the appointment of 2nd Staff Officer to the Column that Colonel Mansfield Clarke was organising at Port Durnford for the purpose of hunting down Cctewayo. It was a great piece of luck, and fortunately the Colonel had no objection to my going, though I'm afraid it inconvenienced him a little, my leaving again so soon after rejoining. Not knowing what arrangements our Brigadier was making with regard to our feeding, I took with me a fairly substantial supply of tinned meat. jam, etc. in case of accidents. Colonel Mansfield Clarke, however, had made ample arrangements, as the Admiral, who was a great friend of his, was on the eve of sailing for Home and had made him a present of enough stores to last several months. All the same, my things came in handy to start off with, and I think pleased the Brigadier, though he said he was sorry that I should have gone to such expense.

I never learned who it was who had so kindly recommended inc for the billet, but on reporting myself, Colonel Clarke received me most kindly, saying that he had heard a good deal about me and hoped that I would keep up the reputation that I had brought. Never was there a stricter or more exacting CO., and never was there a better soldier to serve under, and the result was that the Column worked like clockwork. The Intelligence staff under Captain Murray; R.E., Captain Blood; Mounted

Infantry and Colonial troops, Major Percy Barrow, 19th Hussars; N.N.C., Captain Barton, 7th Royal Fusiliers; Mule battery, Major Duncan, R.A.; Major Tufnell, 3rd/60th Rifles; Major Tredenick, 57th Regiment; Major Tucker, 80th Regiment; Commander Reeves, A.S.G.; Sergeant-Major Giraud, R.A.M.C.; Captain Hart, 81st Regiment. Myself as Staff Officer, and Lieutenant Towers-Clarke, 57th Regiment, orderly officer, made up the Column, not forgetting Jim, who ingratiated himself with everyone and became quite a character in his regimental get-up.

Towers-Clarke and I had all our meals with the Brigadier in his tent - Captain Hart preferring to live separately. "Towers" and I shared a tent, which was always pitched by the side of the Brigadier's.

Our first objective was Ulundi, where Sir Garnet Wolseley had taken up temporary headquarters, and all went well till we reached Entonjaneni, a high hill some fifteen or twenty miles from Ulundi, on the top of which Lord Chelmsford had encamped the night before the battle. But very fortunately for us our Brigadier preferred to camp on the plains at the foot of it, for during the night a terrific hurricane accompanied by a deluge of rain came on, which swept over the whole of Natal, simply devastating the country and completely demolishing our camp. When daylight came, the scene was one of vast desolation, only one tent in the whole camp was left standing and that was the Brigadier's which Captain Hart, Towers-Clarke, myself, our servant and Jim had held on to all night by means of extra ropes and constant hammering in of pegs. How we managed it, I don't know, but we did it, which was the great thing. I can only say it was the worst night I ever spent in my life, and I think I might say with certainty that not a living soul in that camp but would not have expressed the same sentiments. Many of the tents had been blown to ribbons, and some carried off for miles. Cactus and other trees were rooted up everywhere, but the most serious of the damage that was done was the loss of over 300 oxen, which lay dead in their spans by the side of their wagons, which of course meant that until they could be replaced the Column was at a standstill. The tent that Towers-Clarke and I shared, with all our belongings… had completely disappeared, and it was only after hours of searching that, bit by bit, we recovered most of our things again - and in a nice state they were.

Several buck were caught during the night by men of the different Regiments as they were being blown through the camps, and how it was that Major Barrow managed to prevent the ponies and mules of his mounted troops from stampeding was a miracle.

By way of digression, Captain Moir, of my regiment, told me a good story with reference to this same storm which swept away the camp where he was at the time, further down the coast. Private Geoghegan, an Irishman, the Company Cook, determined that his company should not go without their "gun fire" tea, sat on a pot over the fire all night and kept it going - for which thoughtful expedient he got a sovereign! It was the only bit of fire in the camp.

Interior of a Zulu Kraal on the Tugela River.

This crushing loss of oxen of course greatly exercised the Brigadier's mind, and it was a lucky thing for us that the Commander-in-Chief was so close at hand, as he at once directed the officer commanding at Fort Victoria, which was only a few miles off, to hand over all his cattle to our Column, an item which was anything but appreciated by the troops at the Fort. This enabled us, after a little over a week of uncommonly stiff work, digging huge, deep trenches and burying the dead animals, to move on to Ulundi. Here we were hung up for a considerable time, why I can't remember, but there was plenty of work to be clone and in the course of my duties I became well acquainted with General Sir Pomeroy Colley, the Chief of the Staff, and Colonel Eastlake, Deputy Q..M. General.

In my spare time I went over the battlefield of Ulundi and picked up one or two relics in the shape of shields, assegais, etc. A few days after we arrived, Jim came to me to say that he knew the spot where Cetewayo's crown and other paraphernalia presented to him on the occasion of his Coronation by "Somtseu" were buried, and asked if he might go and make a search. I told him certainly, but I would like to go with him, but he said that he would rather go at first by himself and if he found that they had not been taken away he would go with me to get them. However, it turned out that they had been removed, and squatting down, snapping his fingers to emphasise matters, he declared that it had only been done that very day, as the earth from the hole was quite fresh. I should much like to have gone with him afterwards, to have a look at the spot, but I never got the chance.

Several small expeditions consisting of officers and men acting independently were traversing the country in the hope of capturing Cetewayo, and as it seemed likely that our Column would be at Ulundi for some little time, Captain Stewart, 3rd Dragoon Guards, who had joined us on special service, came to my tent one afternoon and told me that if he could get Sir

Garnet Wolseley's sanction he proposed to start an expedition of his own, consisting of officers only, to hunt for Cetewayo, and asked if I would come as Interpreter. Needless to say, I said that I should be only too delighted, if Colonel Clarke would allow it, and I also begged that my co-Adjutant, Towers-Clarke, might be one of the party; to which he agreed. Happily, both Sir Garnet Wolseley and Colonel Mansfield Clarke quite fell in with Stewart's venture, and the following officers formed the expedition:

Captain Stewart, the Chief; myself, Interpreter; Lieutenants Hutton, Smith and (name forgotten) 3/60th; Lieutenant Shepherd, 80th; and Towers-Clarke, 57th Regiment. We took no food of any sort with us, intending to live on what we could get or find at the Kaffir kraals, but Stewart carried a flask of brandy in case of accidents. Our transport consisted of a mule and my Helpmekaar pony to carry cooking utensils, blankets, etc. The mule had to be led, and all except Stewart and I took their turn at this, and a nice lot of trouble he gave us on many occasions. My pony either followed like a clog or was driven along with a whip. Our time was limited to three weeks, when the Column would be on the move again. On the day of our departure, Major McCalmont, 7th Hussars, and I think it was Lieutenant Creagh, R.A., two of Sir Garnet's A.D.C.'s, turned up and said that they were coming with us. But the first night out, with only boiled pumpkin for dinner and nothing but boiled mealies to look forward to the next day, so damped their ardour that when we continued our journey at daybreak they decided to return to camp - and were considerably well chaffed on their sudden change of mind.

First of all we headed towards St. Lucia Bay, travelling over some beautiful country and coming across lots of game, buck, zebra, buffalo, etc. We had a rifle and a few rounds of ammunition with us, our only armament, but reserved it for use only if we got hard up for food, otherwise had we been on a shooting expedition we could have had some splendid sport. Being still at war, nearly all the kraals we visited in the hope of learning something of Cetewayo's whereabouts were denuded of men, none but the very old and the women and children remained, and from these neither information or supplies of any sort could be obtained. When we asked for milk, etc., the invariable reply was, "How are we to get milk when our men are all away fighting?" However, we always got as much food in the shape of mealies and Kaffir corn as we required, by opening the pits in the centre of the cattle kraals (where they always store their crops) and by picking up an odd pumpkin now and again in the fields, all of which we paid for to avoid trouble of any sort.

Only at one kraal not far from the Coast, after we had been out for about a week, did we find not only signs of abundance but also a considerable amount of activity. It was a very large kraal, and a great number of Kaffir women were continually leaving it all the time we were there, laden with baskets of food, most of which, we noticed, was cooked. This raised our hopes considerably, as we felt certain that the supplies must be for the King's party, and a careful watch was kept on the direction the women went. There were several men at the kraal, too, but they showed no signs of hostility in any way and gave us all we wanted except information about the whereabouts of the King, concerning which they pleaded absolute ignorance. It was at this kraal that I obtained the wooden milk pail now at Curtiss's.

Sleeping the night there, we decided to follow the route the women had been taking, and made our way across country towards the junction of the White and Black Umfolozi Rivers. Nothing more was seen of any parties of women, and we very soon lost trace of their tracks in the broken country we passed over. It was a three or four days' journey to the river, and from the numerous kraals we visited en route not a word could we learn about the King's whereabouts in any shape or form.

The morning we reached the Umfolozi, where we had to find a crossing for ourselves, the recognised drifts being some miles away, we had rather an amusing but at the same time a rather uncomfortable experience. After choosing a spot, we first of all had to clear a space through the thick mass of reeds that bordered the river's edge and make a sort of roadway into the water for the ponies, and having nothing but our pocket knives to cut them down it was a long business. Then the next thing was to get our animals over it, but none of them would face it, my pony taking to his heels for all he was worth with half of our belongings on his back. He went a long way up the stream, and it took ages to catch him again. Eventually, however, after much persuasion and a tremendous lot of bother, all were got across except the mule who carried the other half of our traps. He absolutely refused to budge an inch. Coaxing, whacking, shoving, hauling were all tried with no effect, when someone hit on the brilliant idea of cutting a lot of monkey-rope, of which there was any quantity, climbing up the high trees, and twisting it into a miniature cable long enough to pass round him and reach well into the river, so that some of us could get in and pull while others shoved from behind. At last we got him into the water, when he went along without much trouble till about halfway across. Then, without any warning, he suddenly took it into his head to lie down, with the result that our blankets, pots and pans, etc. all went under water.

The only thing we could do now was to unload our traps midstream, carry them piecemeal to the opposite bank and put them to dry as quickly as possible in the sun, and as the animal still remained immovable we fastened one end of the coil of monkey-rope round his neck and, passing the other end round the trunk of a tree on the bank, pulled him up on his legs and literally dragged him out. It was impossible to help laughing after the whole thing was over, but we had had a most uncomfortable experience. Luckily, our blankets soon dried, so we were all right for the night.

A more beautiful spot than the point at which we crossed could not be well imagined, a long stretch of still water bordered with thick masses of feathery reeds and overhung by magnificent trees whose branches almost touched the water. Add to this the delicious scent of some of the flowering shrubs, and the bird life, with the warm atmosphere and wild peacefulness of the surroundings, and you could not wish for anything better or more heavenly.

The next day, one of the first kraals we visited belonged to a hunchback Induna, probably, if not for certain, the only born-so deformity in Zululand who was looked upon with great reverence by the Zulus. He owed his life to the fact that his birth as a deformity had been predicted by the Witchdoctors, who had also foretold that he was to become a powerful chief. Consequently, he was not, as is the invariable custom, put out of the way at birth.

We were now not far from the kraal of Somkele, and had a most unforgettably adventurous day. The country now was almost treeless, and we rode over nothing but a sea of rolling, grassy hills. As we were about to visit a chief almost as powerful as Cetewayo himself, and one who Cetewayo really feared, Stewart, who had brought a white mackintosh with him, put it on despite the heat, to distinguish his dress from ours. He and I usually rode together a little distance ahead of the others, and when we were within a mile or so of Somkele's abode a large party of Zulus appeared coming towards us over a distant rise, fully armed with assegais and shields, which didn't look at all pleasant. When they got to within a few hundred yards of us, just as they were topping some rising ground, they suddenly discarded their assegais, slipping them under the long grass. Stewart didn't quite notice this, but I did, knowing the trick well.

When we met, they carried nothing but their shields, and a couple of indunas came up to us and explained that they had been sent by Somkele to ask what we were doing in his territory. Stewart then informed them that he was on a mission from the Great

Queen and required an interview with Somkele, and that our mission was a peaceful one. Seeing that we were unarmed I think put them at their ease, and we asked them to conduct us to the kraal. But before going on, we asked the Indunas why their men had left their assegais behind in the grass, and told them that we had seen them throwing them away, to which they replied that we must have been mistaken, so we said, "All right, we will take you to the spot", and on getting to the place, there were the assegais, all beautifully hidden. "Now", we said, "How do you account for this?" "Oh", they replied, "We know nothing about it. These must be assegais belonging to the herd boys." "Well", we said, "You must have them all picked up at once, before we go any further." And a goodly lot were collected.

This having been satisfactorily accomplished, we sent the party back to the kraal with a message to Somkele to say that a representative of the Great Queen had come to see him and wished to have a talk with him. In an instant the whole party bounded off like a herd of springbuck, in a great state of delight, apparently, at carrying the news. Deeming it wise to take precautions in case of accidents, Stewart arranged that he and I, on arrival at the kraal, should carry on the preliminaries and while so doing the others of our party should take up positions round the outside and watch for any hostile movements.

The kraal had an enormous circumference, and contained a great number of huts in double rows, the centre space being quite 200 yards wide, if not more. The whole being enclosed with a thick, thorny *zereba*. As we rode up to the entrance gate, which was only a wooden hurdle to keep the cattle out, hundreds of heads peeped over the *zereba* to watch our arrival. We were met almost at once by one of Somkele's Indunas and told that he was too ill to receive us. This, of course, was nonsense, and we sent in a message to say that we were sorry to hear that he was ill, but that as the representative of the Great Queen could not possibly leave without having had an interview with him, we hoped that he would make it convenient to see us. For quite a couple of hours messages were bandied backward and forward to the effect that he couldn't see us and that we insisted on seeing him, when presently the gate was removed and we were informed that Somkele was prepared to receive us.

I shall not forget the scene in a hurry. A roadway led straight through to the top end of the kraal, on either side of which squatted at least 1 000 warriors in full fighting costume. Through these Stewart (with his mackintosh on) and I rode, and as we did so an audible murmur - whether of approval or not, I cannot say - ran through their ranks. Beyond them, at the end of the road, sat Somkele, with an old worsted shawl of many colours thrown over his shoulders and surrounded by his Ministers and Indunas. Having saluted him, he simply waved his hand at us and said, "Get down." However, on looking round I saw that no mats had been placed for us, and mentioned the fact to Stewart, so we said, "When you have provided a place for us, we will get off our horses",

Zulu huts.

and pointed out that the bare ground was not quite the place for a representative of the Great Queen to be asked to take a seat.

Royal mats were at once brought out, and we got off our ponies, which were immediately taken away. We were now absolutely in Somkele's hands, to treat us as he wished. It must be remembered that we were still at war with the Zulu nation, so that it was impossible to say what situation might arise. Just as we were on the point of settling down, up tramped one of Somkele's chiefs from a neighbouring kraal (accompanied by several Indunas, who had, no doubt, been hastily summoned for the occasion), and took his place by Somkele's side. A more magnificent specimen of humanity it would be impossible to conceive. Much over six feet in height, powerfully and perfectly built, and as straight as a dart. Somkele, too, was a fine specimen, but had become fat and unwieldy-looking.

With the arrival of the lastcomer the company was evidently complete, as *utshwala* was handed round and a nice bowlful handed to us after Somkele had had a good pull out of it himself, as is the etiquette, to show that it had not been tampered with. As soon as an opportunity presented itself, Stewart explained to Somkele that it would be better if we could discuss our affairs with him alone and not in the presence of Chiefs and Indunas, which rather alarmed him, I think, at first, but in the end he was good enough to send away everyone except one or two of his special Ministers, which was more than we really expected. It was rather a delicate matter starting the subject of the whereabouts of his uncle, but with Stewart's diplomacy, although the interview was a long one, the discussion was carried on throughout in the most amicable manner. Somkele was a past master in the art of evading compromising questions, and we utterly failed in getting any information out of him.

On the conclusion of the interview Stewart, who always had very grand ideas, said to me, "Harford, we will hold a levée", and the officers who were outside were sent for and formally introduced, the difference in their uniform being explained as Somkele wanted to know why we were not all dressed alike. As each officer was presented, old Somkele felt the cloth of their uniform and in one case said, "Give me that coat", but of course was told that that was impossible as none of us had any other change of clothing. The levee over, Stewart produced his silver flask with the brandy, and offered Somkele a drink. The old chap quickly grabbed at it and took a good pull, exclaiming, "Canteen! Oh! *Umnandi impela*". Then, handing it to each of his ministers in turn without losing hold of it, and only just enabling them to get a taste, polished off the remainder himself, smacking his lips and informing Stewart that he intended to keep the flask, carefully stowing it away behind him. This was awkward, but after a great deal of explanation that it was a gift and could not be parted with, was eventually given up.

During this time one of Somkele's warriors came up and asked if any of us had been at Isandhlwana, and on telling him that I was out with the Contingent at Isipezi at the time of the fight, he caught hold of both my hands and shook them firmly in a great state of delight, saying it was a splendid fight. "You fought well, and we fought well", he exclaimed, and then showed me eleven wounds that he had received, bounding off in the greatest ecstasy to show how it all happened. Rushing up towards me, he jumped, fell on his stomach, got up again, rolled over and over, crawled flat, bounded on again, and so forth, until he came right up to me. His movements being applauded by the warriors squatting in the centre of the kraal with aloud "Gee!"

I now had a look at his wounds. One bullet had gone through his hand, three had gone through his shoulder and had smashed his shoulder-blade, two had cut the skin and slightly into the flesh right down the chest and stomach, and one had gone clean through the fleshy part of the thigh. The others were mere scratches in comparison with these, but there he was, after about eight months, as well as ever and ready for another set-to. Could anything more clearly show the splendid spirit in which the Zulus fought us? No animosity, no revengeful feeling, but just sheer love of a good fight in which the courage of both sides could be tested, and it was evident that the courage of our soldiers was as much appreciated as that of their own.

To compensate Somkele for not letting him keep the brandy flask, Stewart presented him with a round, metal-backed 3d looking-glass and a razor strop, which by the merest chance he happened to have in his pockets. The glass delighted the old chap beyond everything, and at once he held it up close to his face to have a look at himself, and exclaimed, "Ow! I never knew that I was so ugly!" Except for a large mole on his chin, out of which grew a single curly hair, his face was quite smooth, and of this hair he was particularly proud and sat there gently pulling it, with the glass held close up to it for a long time.

It was now getting late and we thought we had better be moving on, and before doing so Stewart asked for a couple of guides to accompany us for a few days, which request, after some little hesitation, was acceded to. Just as we were about to start a small procession of mostly *izintombe* (girls) and one or two youths made their appearance bringing a beautiful cow, two sheep, a couple of goats, and several baskets of mealies and pumpkins as a present for Stewart's acceptance, and at the same time Somkele placed his old kraal, which was some three or four miles away, at our disposal for the night as no-one was living there. Everything was gratefully accepted, and we departed, leaving the guides to join us in the morning.

By the time we reached the kraal a thick, misty drizzle had developed, but we found no difficulty in shaking ourselves down most comfortably in a splendidly roomy and beautifully-built hut, as well as finding excellent shelter for the animals. The remarkably friendly and hospitable manner in which Somkele had received and treated us made us a little suspicious, however, of his real intentions, so we took all the precautions we could in case of accidents, by keeping our ponies saddled and by two of us doing sentry over the hut while Stewart slept and the rest of us patrolled the vicinity throughout the night. But kindly Providence had been with us, and we had belied the good will of our host.

Travelling on now, we continued our search for any sort of information we could get as to Cetewayo's whereabouts, visiting all the kraals where it was at all likely we might get in touch with him. One day we really thought he was in our hands. The kraal was evidently a rich one, and the few men and numerous women about resented every attempt on our part to examine any of the huts, and made an awful fuss. At the hut that I went to look into, a very dear old Kaffir lady, a particularly handsome woman with beautifully fine features, quite unlike a Kaffir and with snow-white hair, sat in the doorway and absolutely refused to move or let me look in till, by dint of a great deal of persuasion, and the assurance that I had no desire to leave the kraal till we had made certain that they were not harbouring the King, she got up and allowed me to have a look. No trace, however, of the King could be found, but in several of the huts a good many guns and other weapons were stowed away, and these we ordered to be collected and taken at once to Headquarters at Ulundi.

Another day, on reaching a kraal where we intended to sleep the night, Stewart and I were lying on the ground just at the edge of the *zereba* outside, cooking our meal, when only a few feet from us, stretched almost at full length in the dried scrub, was a snake that I had often heard of and much wanted to see, and that very few white men have ever come across. It was the *Idhlozi* of the Kaffirs, a beautiful creature, vivid green with jet black marking, between two and three feet long, and thick like a puffadder. I would have given anything to have been able to bottle it, and the opportunity was such as could scarcely ever occur again, no Kaffirs, either men or women, being about. Being held sacred, and looked upon as the incarnation of some ancestor of the kraal, to kill one, if it became known, would certainly mean an assegai put through you, so having no collecting material we left our friend alone.

By a curious coincidence, one morning a day or two after leaving Somkele's, three if not four of the expeditionary parties that were out passed within sight of each other, only a few miles apart. But only Major Maurice, R.A., accompanied by an orderly, came up to us, and this worthy, having pumped us with regard to our movements, put spurs to his horse and rode off, declining to give us any further information than that he had got very reliable news as to Cetewayo's whereabouts. The execrations that followed him as he went off can be imagined. Stewart, who knew his character, could only say, "That's Maurice all over!"

We were then in what is known as "Lion Country", and heard afterwards that one of the parties had lost three horses that night, which had been killed and dragged several hundred yards from their bivouac to be eaten.

It was very evident that the various expeditions had been following much the same scent, and no doubt their movements concerning which Cetewayo was kept well informed, led him to take refuge in the Ngome forest where eventually "Clarke's Column" succeeded in capturing him. Our three weeks nearing to the end, we began working our way back to Ulundi, visiting kraals en route to search for arms and giving orders wherever we found any for them to be taken to Headquarters as we had no means of breaking them up.

On the day we were due to rejoin the Column, Towers-Clarke and I picked up our two servants and a mule cart left for us at a point some little distance from Ulundi, as the Column had gone on. Here Stewart and the other officers parted from us; we had had a most delightful and adventurous journey of some 300 miles over most wonderfully picturesque country, depending on Providence for food, while still at war with its inhabitants, always, except on one occasion, sleeping in the open veld and never once seeing any sign of hostility.

Being late in the afternoon, and no chance of reaching the Column that night as there was no road and we had nothing to guide us as to the route the Column had taken, (except when the grass had been trodden down by the troops and here and there wagon tracks on the hard soil), we decided to drive on till it was dark and get on again at dawn. We had the advantage of half moon for a short while, and as that set we hauled up under a lovely flat-crown tree for the night. Here, while our servants were taking the traps out of the cart, the mules being unharnessed, and Towers-Clarke and I arranging our bivouac, I saw a large animal which I took to be a wolf coming steadily down from a knoll close to us, and pointed it out to Towers. Then, as it was too dark to see clearly, and being curious to know what sort of animal it was, I stole very quietly towards it and stood perfectly still to watch. Presently, as it got nearer, I saw it was a lioness, and called to Towers to let me have one of our servants' rifles as quickly as he could. In the meantime she had walked up to within a yard of me, and I could have almost caught hold of her. There she stood with her great eyes looking from side to side, not taking the slightest notice of me.

The servants, having very foolishly laid their rifles at the bottom of the cart, were unable to get them out till everything had been unloaded, and long before that had been done, Her Majesty had quietly walked off. However, I carefully watched the direction she had gone in, and presuming that she had not gone far, as undoubtedly it was the mules that she was after, as soon as I got hold of a rifle I went off and lay down where I thought I might get a shot as she circled round. I did fire at something that I thought looked like an animal moving in the grass in front of me against the skyline, but when we went to look round before we started in the morning, saw nothing even like a track in the grass. It would have been a splendid thing if we could have arrived in camp with a lioness in our cart, and most certainly we should have done so if the men's rifles had been handy.

Our Column was now following no specified route, consequently an enormous amount of road-clearing had to be done, especially over streams and vleis as with ox-wagons a good semicircular sweep is required for the long spans of oxen to work round and get the strain to enable them to pull the wagon straight across. The Intelligence officer, who always kept a day ahead of the Column, selected the route and sent his sketch-map in every evening with all bad places specially marked, and it was my duty to go off each morning at daybreak with a company of one of the regiments, suitably equipped with axes, shovels, etc., to get these bad places put straight before the Column came up. I enjoyed the work immensely, and if only it had been possible to combine sport with duty could have bagged numbers of guineafowl and partridge. At one vlei in particular, I remember, the party had been working for several hours and just as they had finished out flew quite forty or fifty guineafowl from a thickly covered tree, close above our heads.

As a rule our company grounds were reached about eleven o'clock, and occasionally one was able to get out with the gun. One afternoon Major Duncan, R.A. and I took a turn out to look for buck, and on beating down a ravine where he was one side and I on the other, I saw his spaniel working very excitedly in a thick bit of scrub a little way behind him, and called out to him to look out as I thought that there was something there. In a few minutes the dog jumped out, uttering a little whine as if he had pricked himself in the thorns, and we went on. Then, as we got further down the dog lagged behind considerably, and I said to Duncan, "Your dog is a long way behind. I think he's got a prickle in his foot, as I heard him whine as he got out of that bush. We'd better go back and see." So we went back, and found his head all swollen and a trickle of blood running from the tip of his nose. Seeing at once that he had been bitten by a snake, Duncan took him in his arms and I carried the guns and we made for the camp as hard as we could go.

By the time we got in, the animal's head was quite the size of a football, his eyes were closed up and his tongue an enormous size. Duncan at once got his medicine-chest and produced a bottle of salvolatile, rubbing some on his nose, and with the greatest difficulty getting some down his throat. We continued this treatment every now and then till the last thing at night, adding an occasional drop of milk. For three or four days the dog remained in a state of stupor, but eventually pulled through all right - most probably it was a Mamba that had bitten him. Had it been a Puffadder it is improbable that he would have recovered.

The Column worked its way along in accordance with the reports received from various quarters by the Intelligence department, until one morning a Kaffir arrived at our bivouac and informed the Brigadier that he knew the place in the Ngome bush where Cetewayo was hiding, and could show him the way to the kraal. Young Oftebro, our interpreter, who was the son of a missionary and who had lived among the Zulus all his life, knew the country well and was also a personal friend of Cetewayo's, so without any delay Colonel Mansfield Clarke sent him off to accompany a squadron of the King's Dragoon Guards under Major Marter and a company of N.N.C. under Captain Barton, Royal Fusiliers, to effect the King's capture. When the party had started, I shall never forget the kind way in which Colonel Clarke said to me, "You know, Harford, I would have sent you, but Oftebro knows every inch of the country as well as the King himself, and his thorough knowledge of the language is most important", (or words to that effect).

The fact of Major Marter's party capturing Cetewayo was a great blow to Lord Gifford's expedition, which had run him to earth and were on the point of bagging him, but not knowing the lie of the country had got to a place where they couldn't move without being seen by day and were holding on till it got dark. Marter's party, being led by experts, took a route completely concealing their movements, almost under Gifford's nose, and rapidly surrounding the kraal captured him. In telling me the story afterwards, Oftebro said that as soon as the kraal had been surrounded and our troops were closing in on it, one or two shots were fired, but Cetewayo saw that the game was up. He himself then went up to the hut that the King was in, and spoke to him from outside, and directly Cetewayo heard his voice he said, "Is that you?"… (calling him by his Zulu name), and after a few minutes' conversation, quietly gave himself up.

At dawn, almost at the first streak of light the following morning, a Kaffir messenger from Major Marter appeared with a note fastened in the slit of a small stick. The Brigadier, Towers-Clarke and I were sleeping under our wagon. The Brigadier lay between us, I being on the outside. On handing me the stick, the bearer whispered, very quietly, "He is caught!", and I woke the Brigadier, handing him the stick without a word. "Marter's got him", he said, as he jumped up, and went off to tell the news to Captain Hart, and in a very few minutes it was known throughout the camp. A cart had also been asked for, for the conveyance of the King and his wives, which was immediately sent off under the guidance of the messenger. On the way in, I believe, some of the followers gave a lot of trouble and had to be fastened to the troopers' horses, but eventually all arrived safely. On arrival in camp, the sight of so many soldiers alarmed them considerably, and Cetewayo looked the picture of fright as they drove up. After alighting from the cart, the King (with his wives hanging on to him as if they thought he was doomed to immediate execution, and absolutely terrified), strode in with the aid of his long stick, with a proud and dignified air and grace, looking a magnificent specimen of his race and every inch a warrior in his grand *umutcha* of leopard skin and tails, with lion's teeth and claw charms round his neck. Well over six feet, fat but not corpulent, with a stern, severe and cruel countenance, he looked what he was, a savage ruler.

A tent was provided for him and his wives, and a guard mounted over it of the 60th Rifles, and for the two days he remained in camp Colonel Clarke very kindly paid me the compliment of giving them over into my charge. After that, they were driven to Maritzburg in a mule wagon in charge of Lieutenant Poole, R.A., with a mounted escort. Cetewayo had brought with him when he came in two very nice grass baskets filled with *utshwala*, and on his departure I handed one to Colonel Clarke, and the other I brought home, (the last he drank out of), and gave to Dr Ray.

Having captured the King and thus virtually ended the campaign, the Column had to see the completion of the surrendering of

'Cetewayo in captivity' by Harford.
(London Illustrated News)

arms, demanded and ordered by the Government. One powerful and recalcitrant chief, Sibebu , gave us a lot of trouble, doing all he possibly could to evade the authorities. At last, after repeated demands, the Brigadier sent him a message to say that if his orders were not complied with by a certain day and hour, troops would be sent to enforce them. On the day and hour named, as no Sibebu or arms were forthcoming, Major Marter's squadron of the King's Dragoon Guards, accompanied by the Brigadier himself with me as Staff Officer (and last, but not least Jim, who had begged to be allowed to come out), rode off towards Sibebu's kraal to give him a fright. Having gone some three or four miles, a swarm of Kaffirs, some of them mounted, could be seen in the distance coming towards us, so we halted to await their arrival.

Just as they topped a hill rising in front of us, a most ridiculous scene occurred. Sibebu and his mounted escort were riding a little distance ahead of the men bringing in the arms, and as they came over the rise Major Marter gave the command to his men to mount,

Major Marter and his men guarding Cetewayo in the native kraal.

and these quickly wheeled to the right, so as to face the Zulus. The movement, being so suddenly and quickly executed, so alarmed Sibebu and his mounted followers that the whole lot of them either fell or scrambled off their ponies, imagining, no doubt, that our men were going to charge. It was very funny, and impossible to keep from laughing. On seeing that our troops remained in position, Sibebu came up to Colonel Clarke and offered all sorts of excuses for not having delivered up the arms before, but the Brigadier gave him very; clearly to understand what he thought of his conduct.

Now followed a little incident which I was quite unprepared for. Jim came quietly up, and asked if he might be allowed to speak to Sibebu. This rather astounded me, and Colonel Clarke having no objection the two greeted each other most cordially, snuffed together and showed every sign of intimate acquaintance. Jim told me later on that he was his brother-in-law, having married one of his sisters. It was a curious coincidence their coming together again in this way.

Now that Sibebu had been successfully dealt with, the Column's mission was at an end, and in accordance with orders from Headquarters we proceeded to Maritzburg for dispersal - and a very pleasant march it was, passing over a lovely country, via Kwamagwaza English Mission Station and Greytown. From one of our camps we were only a few miles from Eshowe, so I took a hurried ride up to have a look at the place and find poor Davison's grave and get a sketch of it.

Just to show one of the barbarous customs practised by the Zulus, I give an incident, gruesome as it is, which occurred at our Kwamagwaza camp. As is the case in all campaigns, a certain number of animals have to be left behind when the troops march off, being too exhausted to go on. As a rule… they revive and soon pick up again, when sometimes they are driven in and more often than not are annexed by the people who find them. Three or four had to be discarded at Kwamagwaza. For some reason, (I forget now what), some short time after the Column had marched I had to return to the camping-ground, and as I rode in I saw clumps of Kaffirs sitting round the oxen that we had been unable to take on. I went up to see what they were about, thinking that they had despatched them and were going to have a feast, but to my horror found that they were calmly carving out a large shield from the back of each ox and skinning it off while the poor beasts were still alive, some extraordinary superstition being attached to this particular method of obtaining a shield! Having a good hunting-crop with me, I used it pretty freely on one or two that I rode down, but this was useless as directly I got out of sight again they would only be back again like vultures to carry on with their work. The only consolation one had was that within an hour or two they would all be slaughtered and by the following morning nothing but their bones left.

Nothing more being required of me after arrival at Maritzburg, I rejoined my Regiment at Pinetown, where they and the 24th Regiment were encamped on the open ground just outside the boundaries of our old farm, *Stapleton Grove*. Jim and I parted at Maritzburg with many regrets on both sides, I to rejoin the 99th and he to return to his kraal.

A copy of Colonel Mansfield Clarke's farewell orders to his staff is in one of my boxes at Curtiss's, and when personally wishing him goodbye, he very kindly said that if ever he could be of any use to me, to be sure and let him know. I owe a very great deal to his kindness when he became Adjutant-General at the War Office, later on.

We remained at Pinetown for a considerable time, awaiting orders, and eventually embarked on the 31st December, for Bermuda.

While at Pinetown I was able to renew many old acquaintanceships and visit old shooting and collecting haunts.

The features of the country round about were not much changed, except that many springs and streams had dried up and notably the Umbilo River, which was the boundary of the side of our farm, and the beautiful rivulet which ran into it from the other. A very amusing incident took place a few days after I arrived in the camp, when our old friend known as "Drunken Davidson" came to pay me a visit. It was just at our orderly-room hour, when prisoners, orderly N.C.O.'s and others were waiting for the Colonel to arrive, that a wild horseman came charging into the camp, shouting at the top of his voice, "I want to see Mr. Charles Harford!", repeating this many times over. He was told by the Sergeant-Major that I was in the orderly-room tent and very busy. However, recognising my old friend's voice, for many scores of times when a boy he had woken me up at all hours of the night shouting almost the same words, I went out to greet him. To the great amusement of the assembled officers, N.C.O.'s and men, he fell on my neck and kissed and hugged me and shouted out his joy at meeting the son of Captain Charles Harford once more, making all sorts of grimaces and roaring with laughter and joking as was his wont.

At this moment Major Walker, who was doing the Colonel's work that morning, (and to whom I had often related stories of old Davidson's wild escapades), came up, and taking in the situation asked him to take a seat in the tent and wait till I had finished my work and orderly-room was over. So he stalked in and sat down at my table at the back of the tent, as quiet as a mouse, with one arm leaning on the table and looking very wise. Presently, seeing my glengarry cap on the table, he at once put it on, and as this could be seen by everyone outside, even the prisoners couldn't help laughing. It caused the CO. to look round and see what the joke was about, and he also couldn't help smiling and chuckling to himself. The whole scene was most ridiculous, but to appreciate it one wants to have seen the man and watched his monkey-like sudden changes of countenance and facial expression. Directly I was free I took him to my tent, where we talked over old times and, after tossing off half a tumbler of neat whisky, he galloped off to give someone else a treat.

In 1881, after having been eighteen months in Bermuda, we were suddenly ordered to South Africa for service against the Boers, but on reaching Cape Town found that peace had been declared. The Regiment was sent into camp at Wynberg, which at that time was one of the most beautiful spots in Cape Colony, and except for the few farms and vineyards in the vicinity remained in a state of nature.

Here I was able to renew my acquaintance with Cetewayo, who with his wives was in exile living in a home provided for them by the Government a mile or two out on the Cape Flats - a more or less dreary residence but very comfortable. Occasionally I went out to have a talk with him, which I think he appreciated, and when the Regiment got settled down and band days were instituted, finding that the authorities had no objection, he was given a standing invitation to our weekly "At Homes". This pleased him immensely, particularly as a bottle of champagne was always opened for his special benefit. He was generally the first guest to arrive, and coming early as he did, almost always had to sit with me in our orderly-room while I went on with my work.

On one occasion, when I told him that the High Commissioner and his wife, Sir Hercules and Lady Robinson, were coming, he was greatly excited, and kept on asking when I thought they would arrive, and getting up to look out of the tent when there was anything like the rumble of a trap. The fact was that he had taken a violent fancy to Lady Robinson, who was an uncommonly pretty lady, and rumours were current that he had already made tender enquiries as to whether Sir Hercules would part with her for fifty cows!! Whether this ever reached Lady Robinson's ears I never heard, but no doubt somebody would have told her the joke.

Cetywayo ka Mpande, photograph c.1885.

Cetewayo always took the greatest interest in inspecting the Band instruments and hearing the different sounds that were got out of them, and, greatly to the amusement of the men, went round asking them to blow hard. His favourite instrument was a double bass, to which he invariably placed his ear while the boy who played it blew for all he was worth. Of course at these "At Homes" Cetewayo wore European clothes, which detracted greatly from his appearance as a Monarch; Cetewayo in his Royal savage dress of leopard tails and skins, and Cetewayo in a tailor-made suit of European clothing, were two distinctly different individuals, scarcely to be identified with one another.